Nature of Science • Biological World • Chemical World • Physical

GW00359390

Catalyst
Workbook

**Your companion for change
to the new course**

educate.ie

PUBLISHED BY:

Educate.ie

Walsh Educational Books Ltd
Castleisland, Co. Kerry, Ireland
www.educate.ie

PRINTED AND BOUND BY:
Walsh Colour Print, Castleisland

Copyright © Educate.ie 2017

PHOTOGRAPHS:
Front-cover photograph: Bigstock
ISBN: 978-1-911464-63-1

Contents

Introduction: Nature of Science

Biological World

Chemical World

Nature of Science

Nature of Science

0.1 What is Science?

1. What is science the study of?

   _____

2. Put the steps of the scientific method in the correct order by numbering them 1 to 5.

   Form conclusions   ☐

   Observation (ask a question)   ☐

   Analyse the results   ☐

   Form a hypothesis   ☐

   Test the hypothesis with investigations ☐

3. Give **one** example of a testable hypothesis.

   _____

   _____

4. Give **one** example of an untestable hypothesis.

   _____

   _____

5. Complete the diagram.

6. Explain the difference between a theory and a law/principle.

   _____

   _____

   _____

   _____

   _____

0.2 Investigation Design

1. What is a scientific investigation?

   _____

   _____

2. Explain why it is important to carry out a risk assessment before beginning an investigation.

   _____

   _____

   _____

   _____

   _____

3. What **two** factors must you decide on before carrying out an investigation?

   _____

   _____

4. Tick the correct column to identify the type of variable being described.

	Independent	Dependent	Controlled (fixed)
A variable that changes as a result of changing the independent variable			
A variable that you change			
All the variables that are kept the same			

5. **a.** Identify possible independent, dependent and controlled (fixed) variables in the following investigation.

   > A study to find out how the number of Mentos added to Coke affects the fizziness of the reaction.

   Independent variable: _____

   Dependent variable: _____

   Controlled (fixed) variable: _____

   b. Give an example of a suitable control for this investigation.

   _____

   _____

6. What **two** features must a method have to ensure it is reliable?

   _____

   _____

7. Identify if the following investigations are ethical or unethical and give a reason why.

Investigation	Ethical/unethical	Reason
Testing if the thread depth of tyres affects the stopping distances of cars		
Testing if the number of cups of coffee consumed per day affects a person's reaction times on a computer game		
Testing if a new chocolate bar causes laboratory mice to gain weight and develop diabetes		

0.3 Recording, Presenting and Analysing Data

1. Explain the difference between primary data and secondary data and give **one** example of each.

_____

_____

_____

_____

_____

_____

2. Tick the correct column to identify if the data is qualitative or quantitative.

	Qualitative	Quantitative
The length of your hair		
The colour of your hair		
Your favourite school subject		
The number of subjects you study at school		
The distance you travel to school		
Your method of travelling to school		
Your age		
The month of your birthday		

3. Identify **one** suitable type of graph or chart to present the following data.

Data	Suitable graph or chart
The eye colours of the students in your class	
The students' favourite ice cream flavours	
A student's exam results over a period of time	
Sports played by First Year students	
The methods of travel students use to get to school	
The number of students in each year group	

4. **a.** In the graph below, show a directly proportional relationship between variable A and variable B.

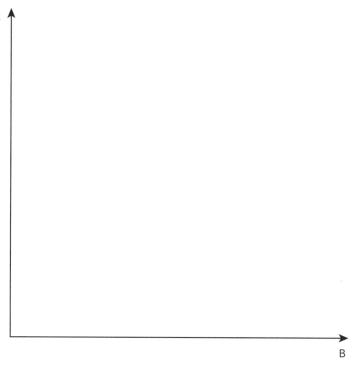

b. In the graph below, show an inversely proportional relationship between variable A and variable B.

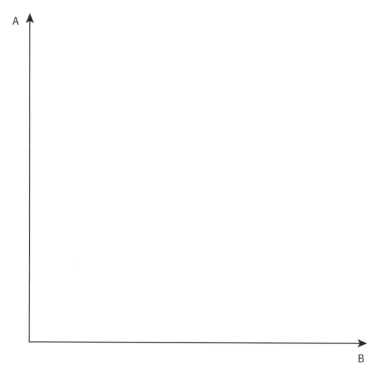

5. Explain what a conclusion is in a scientific investigation.

_____

_____

_____

_____

0.4 Communication, Teamwork and Responsible Science

1. Identify suitable ways to communicate scientific information in the following scenarios (i.e. event, media, journal article or model).

Scenario	Suitable communication method
Explain the active ingredient in a sports drink to possible customers	
Present new findings in cancer research	
Demonstrate the structure of an atom to students	
Showcase advances in virtual reality technology	

2. Explain the term **model** for communicating ideas in science and give **one** example.

_____

_____

_____

_____

3. Identify **three** professional fields of the scientists who contribute to the work at CERN.

_____

_____

_____

4. Explain why it is important to consider who is communicating scientific information.

_____

_____

_____

_____

5. Outline **four** important characteristics of a scientist.

_____

_____

_____

_____

Crossword

Introduction: Nature of Science

Across

1. Carried out by scientists to answer questions about the natural world. (14)
4. Process by which a scientist's work is judged by a team of scientists to ensure it is valid. (4, 6)
6. Data recorded in numbers. (12)
7. Copy of an investigation, in which every factor is the same except the independent variable. (7)
8. Explains and predicts natural phenomena. (6)
9. Formed after a scientist has analysed the results of an investigation. (11)
10. Data recorded using descriptive words. (11)
11. Idea that will be tested by an investigation. (10)

Down

2. Series of steps followed by scientists to investigate testable natural occurrences. (10, 6)
3. Factors that can be changed, measured or controlled in an investigation. (9)
5. Difference between the highest and lowest data values in an investigation. (5)

Biological World

Chapter 1

The Organisation of Life

1.1 Defining Life

1. What is biology the study of?

   _____

2. Complete the following table outlining the seven characteristics of life.

Characteristic	Definition
	Removal of wastes from cells
Reproduction	
	Increase in the size of an organism
	Ability to react to a change in the environment
Respiration	
	Change in an organism's location or position
Nutrition	

3. Explain the difference between excretion and egestion.

   _____

   _____

   _____

4. Why do living things grow?

   _____

5. Describe how the response of a sunflower to the position of the sun in the sky is different from the response of a rabbit to a nearby fox.

   _____

   _____

   _____

6. Why is it important for organisms to be able to respond to changes in their environment?

   _____

1.2 The Cell and Light Microscope

1. What are cells?

   _____

   _____

2. Which scientist is credited with inventing the light microscope?

   _____

3. Explain the difference between unicellular and multicellular organisms. Give **one** example of each.

   _____

   _____

   _____

4. Label the parts of the light microscope.

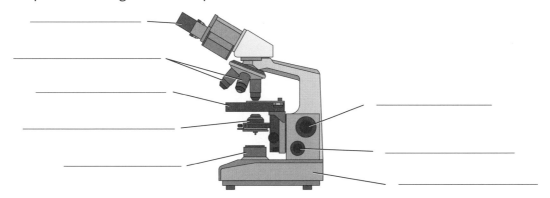

5. Tick the correct column to identify which statements are true and which are false.

	True	False
The coarse focus should be adjusted before the fine focus		
The fine focus should be adjusted before the coarse focus		
Iodine is a suitable stain to use when viewing onion cells		
Methylene blue is a suitable stain to use when viewing plant cells		
If the eyepiece lens is × 10 and the objective lens is × 40, then the total magnification is 50		
If the eyepiece lens is × 10 and the objective lens is × 40, then the total magnification is 400		

6. Does the following microscope image show animal cells or plant cells?

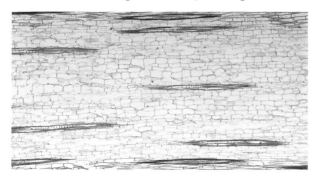

   Answer: _____

1.3 The Structure of the Cell

1. What is an organelle?

   _____

   _____

2. Label the parts of the animal cell.

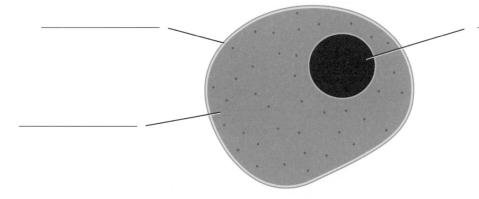

3. Label the parts of the plant cell.

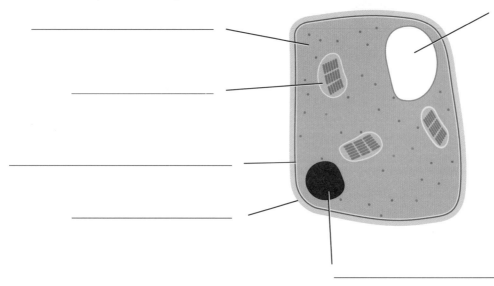

4. Describe the functions of the following organelles.

   a. Nucleus: _____

   _____

   b. Cell membrane: _____

   _____

   c. Cell wall: _____

   _____

5. List **three** differences between an animal cell and a plant cell.

   _____

   _____

   _____

1.4 Organisation of Life

1. Name the building block of all organisms.

   _____

2. Describe what is meant by the term **organisation** when discussing organisms.

   _____

3. Put the levels of organisation in order, starting with the simplest level.

   | Tissue | System | Organelle | Organ | Cell | Organism |

   1. _____
   ↓
   2. _____
   ↓
   3. _____
   ↓
   4. _____
   ↓
   5. _____
   ↓
   6. _____

4. Match each organisational level with its description.

Organisational level	Description
1. Tissue	a. Group of organs that work together
2. Cell	b. Structure with a particular role within a cell
3. Organ	c. Result of all systems working together
4. Organelle	d. Group of cells that work together
5. Organism	e. A group of tissues that work together
6. System	f. Building block of life, made up of organelles

1.	2.	3.	4.	5.	6.

5. Give **one** example of each of the following.
   a. Organelle: _____
   b. Cell: _____
   c. Tissue: _____
   d. Organ: _____
   e. System: _____

Crossword

Chapter 1: The Organisation of Life

Across

1. Sample studied under a microscope. (8)
4. Organisms made up of a single cell. (11)
6. Ability to react to a change in the environment. (8)
8. New individuals produced by reproduction. (9)
9. Living thing. (8)
11. Release of energy from food. (11)
12. Microscope used to view cells in the school laboratory. (5)

Down

2. Controls which materials move in and out of the cell. (4, 8)
3. Image formed by an electron microscope. (10)
5. Jelly-like substance surrounded by the cell membrane. (9)
7. Group of organs that work together. (6)
10. Control centre of the cell. (7)

The Chemicals of Life

2.1 Biomolecules and Food Tests

1. What term is used to describe all of the food consumed by an organism?

   _____

2. Name the **four** biomolecules needed by all organisms.

   _____

   _____

3. Match each biomolecule or nutrient with a function it carries out.

Biomolecules and nutrients		Function	
1.	Minerals	a.	Keeps gums and teeth healthy
2.	Proteins	b.	Regulates temperature
3.	Water	c.	Provides a supply of energy
4.	Vitamins	d.	Assist with chemical reactions
5.	Carbohydrates	e.	Protects internal organs
6.	Fats	f.	Make muscle, hair and enzymes

1.	2.	3.	4.	5.	6.

4. Complete the following table by naming **two** possible food sources of each biomolecule or nutrient.

Biomolecules and nutrients	Food sources
Carbohydrates	
Proteins	
Fats	
Vitamins	
Minerals	
Water	

5. The orange-brown chemical iodine is used to test for the presence of starch in food. Complete the following sentences using the words below.

   > negative   starch   positive   blue-black   milk   iodine

   If a drop of iodine is placed on a potato, the iodine will turn _____. This colour change is a _____ result for _____ in potatoes.

   If a drop of iodine is placed in milk, the _____ will not change colour. This is a _____ result for starch in _____.

2.2 The Importance of a Balanced Diet

1. What is a balanced diet?

   _____

   _____

2. Name **three** factors that should inform a person's dietary choices.

   _____

   _____

   _____

3. Which person needs the highest energy intake and why?

   a. A hockey player *or* a spectator at a match

   _____

   _____

   b. A pregnant office worker *or* her non-pregnant female colleague

   _____

   _____

4. Explain why food labels state typical values per 100 g, even though the product may contain more or less than 100 g?

   _____

   _____

   _____

5. Calculate the BMI of an adult male of height 1.82 m and mass of 77.3 kg.

   _____
   | |
   |_____|

   Answer: _____

6. Explain why BMI is not always a reliable measure of a person's healthy weight status.

   _____

   _____

   _____

7. Based on the food pyramid, match the recommended servings to the food group.

Food group		Recommended servings	
1.	Meat, poultry, eggs, fish and dairy	**a.**	3–4 servings a day
2.	Vegetables	**b.**	3–5 servings a day
3.	Fats, oils, cakes and sweets	**c.**	2–3 servings a day
4.	Breads, cereals, potatoes, rice and pasta	**d.**	Rarely
5.	Fruit	**e.**	6 servings a day

1.	2.	3.	4.	5.

2.3 Malnutrition

1. What is malnutrition?

   _____

2. What is a deficiency disease?

   _____

   _____

3. Complete the following table.

Disease	Dietary and lifestyle cause(s)	Symptom(s)
Type 2 diabetes		
Osteoporosis		
Anaemia		

4. Describe the health risks associated with obesity and suggest a possible solution.

   _____

   _____

   _____

   _____

   _____

   _____

   _____

5. In addition to a balanced diet, identify **four** other lifestyle choices that need to be considered to promote good health.

   _____

   _____

   _____

Crossword

Chapter 2: The Chemicals of Life

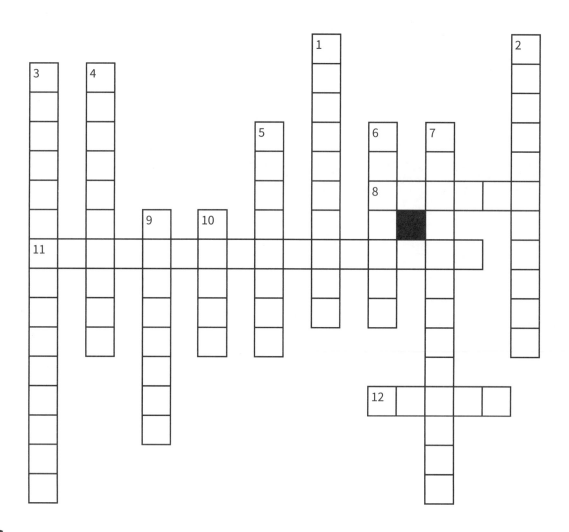

Across

8. Deficiency disease caused by a lack of vitamin C. (6)
11. Provides energy information on food packaging. (11, 5)
12. Carbohydrate that provides a fast supply of energy. (5)

Down

1. Energy in food, measured in thousands of joules. (10)
2. Helps people plan a balanced diet by showing recommended servings of food groups. (4, 8)
3. Values that provide information about the calories, sugar, fat and salt needed for a healthy diet. (9, 6)
4. Caused by a shortage of food. (10)
5. Diet that provides biomolecules in the correct quantities. (8)
6. Condition that affects an organism's ability to work normally. (7)
7. Chemical used to test food for protein. (6, 7)
9. Disease that affects how the body uses glucose. (8)
10. Carbohydrate that keeps the digestive system in good working order. (5)

The Energy of Life

3.1 Metabolism, Enzymes and Homeostasis

1. List **three** reasons why organisms need energy.

   _____

   _____

   _____

2. What is metabolism?

   _____

   _____

3. What is an enzyme?

   _____

   _____

4. Label the following diagram to show the action of an enzyme changing maltose to glucose.

   | Enzyme (maltase)   Product (glucose)   Substrate (maltose)   Enzyme (maltase) |

5. Define the term **homeostasis**.

   _____

   _____

   _____

6. Humans maintain a constant body temperature of 37 °C. Describe how the human body responds to an increase and a decrease in body temperature.

   Increase in body temperature: _____

   _____

   Decrease in body temperature: _____

   _____

3.2 Photosynthesis

1. What is photosynthesis?

   _____

   _____

2. What is the ultimate source of all energy on Earth?

   _____

3. Complete the word equation for photosynthesis.

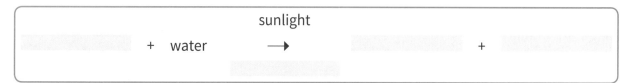

   sunlight

   _____ + water ⟶ _____ + _____

4. Tick the correct column to identify the reactants and products of photosynthesis.

	Reactant	Product
Glucose		
Carbon dioxide		
Oxygen		
Water		

5. Match the reactants and products of photosynthesis to their descriptions.

Reactant/product	Description
1. Chlorophyll	a. Enters through stomata
2. Carbon dioxide	b. Energy absorbed by leaves
3. Glucose	c. Released into the air through stomata
4. Sunlight	d. Green pigment in plant cells
5. Water	e. Food made by the plant
6. Oxygen	f. Enters through the plant's roots

1.	2.	3.	4.	5.	6.

6. Explain why photosynthesis is important to the food industry.

   _____

   _____

   _____

7. Identify **two** ways that a horticulturist or a farmer could adjust the conditions in a glasshouse or polytunnel to increase the rate of photosynthesis.

   _____

   _____

   _____

   _____

3.3 Respiration

1. An organism gets its food in one of two ways. Explain the difference between consumers and producers.

   _____

   _____

   _____

2. What is respiration?

   _____

   _____

   _____

3. In which organelle does respiration take place?

   _____

4. Explain the role of enzymes in respiration.

   _____

   _____

   _____

5. Complete the word equation for respiration.

   ┌───┐
   │   │
   │   +   ⟶   +   +   │
   │   │
   │   .   │
   └───┘

6. Tick the correct column to identify the reactants and products of respiration.

	Reactant	Product
Glucose		
Carbon dioxide		
Oxygen		
Water		

7. Complete the following sentences using the words below.

   ┌───┐
   │ building   photosynthesise   releases   stores   breaking   respire │
   └───┘

   Only some organisms _____ , but all organisms _____ .

   Photosynthesis is a _____ reaction. This means that it temporarily _____ energy.

   Respiration is a _____ reaction. This means that it _____ energy.

8. What chemical is used to test for the presence of carbon dioxide?

   _____

Crossword

Chapter 3: The Energy of Life

Across

2. Made when an enzyme acts on a substrate. (7)
5. Needed for a chemical reaction to take place. (8)
6. Organelle in which respiration takes place. (12)
8. Green pigment in plant cells that absorbs light energy. (11)
9. Substance an enzyme acts on. (9)
10. Biological catalyst that speeds up reactions in cells. (6)
11. Small openings in leaves though which carbon dioxide enters. (7)

Down

1. Form of respiration that requires oxygen. (7)
3. Organisms' quest for 'sameness'. (11)
4. Organism that makes its own food by photosynthesis. (8)
7. Organism that must find and eat food. (8)

Chapter 4

The Continuity of Life: Genetics and Evolution

4.1 Genetics

1. What is genetics?

   _____

   _____

   _____

   _____

2. Tick the correct column to identify the characteristics as inherited or acquired.

Characteristic	Inherited	Acquired
Accent you speak in		
Hair colour		
Ability to drive a car		
Eye colour		
Blood type		
Hair length		
Colour blindness		
Muscle definition from exercise		

3. Where are chromosomes located?

   _____

4. What **two** biomolecules are chromosomes made up of?

   _____

   _____

5. Name the scientists who, in 1953, discovered the structure of DNA.

   _____

6. Complete the following sentences using the words and numbers below.

   | fertilisation | egg | reproduction | 23 | sperm | zygote | 46 |

   Every human body cell contains _____ chromosomes, apart from gametes which contain _____ chromosomes each.

   The male gamete is called a _____ . The female gamete is called an _____ .

   The male and female gametes fuse during _____ and a single cell called a _____ is produced. This is the first step in sexual _____ .

7. Explain how fertilisation results in a unique combination of traits in a child.

_____

_____

_____

_____

_____

_____

8. Tick the correct column to identify which statements are true and which are false.

	True	False
A dominant trait will show in a child if only one parent has the dominant gene		
A recessive trait will show in a child if only one parent has the dominant gene		
A dominant trait will show in a child if both parents have the dominant gene		
A recessive trait will show if both parents have the recessive gene		

9. Explain what is meant by the expression 'nature versus nurture'. Give **one** example.

_____

_____

_____

_____

_____

_____

4.2 Variation and Evolution

1. What is a species?

   _____

   _____

2. Tick the correct column to identify if the variations are influenced by environment, inheritance or both.

	Environment	Inheritance	Both
Eye colour			
Blood group			
Height			
Skin colour			
Weight			
Food preferences			

3. Complete the following sentences using the words below.

   > selection   species   environment   survive   reproduce   generations

   Natural _____ is the process by which the members of a _____
   who are best suited to their _____ are most likely to _____
   and _____ . Any useful changes that take place will be passed on to future
   _____ .

4. Give **one** example of natural selection.

   _____

   _____

5. What is evolution?

   _____

   _____

   _____

6. Give **two** sources of evidence to support Darwin's theory of evolution by natural selection.

   _____

   _____

7. Outline **one** example of the selective breeding of useful characteristics in animals or plants by humans.

   _____

   _____

   _____

   _____

4.3 Mutation

1. What is a mutation?

   _____

   _____

2. Identify **three** environmental factors that may increase the likelihood of a mutation.

   _____

   _____

   _____

3. Explain how a tumour forms.

   _____

   _____

   _____

4. Name **three** mutagens that can increase the possibility of cancer.

   _____

   _____

   _____

5. Explain how a genetic mutation may be passed on to offspring from a parent.

   _____

   _____

   _____

6. Look at the following karyotype.

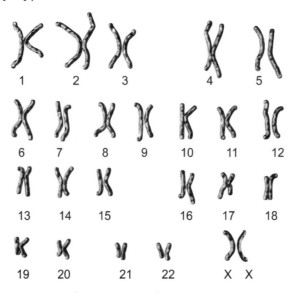

   a. Does it show the chromosomes of a male or a female?

   _____

   b. Does it suggest any genetic disorders in the individual?

   _____

4.4 Genetic Engineering and Cloning

1. What is biotechnology?

   _____

   _____

   _____

   _____

2. Name **two** early examples of biotechnology.

   _____

   _____

3. Name **two** modern industries that have used biotechnology. Give **one** example of its use in each industry.

   _____

   _____

   _____

   _____

   _____

4. What is genetic engineering?

   _____

   _____

   _____

5. Outline how diabetic patients have benefitted from advances in genetic engineering.

   _____

   _____

   _____

   _____

6. Explain the difference between genetic engineering and cloning in terms of the genes produced by each process.

   _____

   _____

   _____

   _____

   _____

   _____

7. Explain the term GM food.

   _____

   _____

   _____

Crossword

Chapter 4: The Continuity of Life: Genetics and Evolution

Across

2. Thread-like structures in the nucleus of animal and plant cells. (11)
4. Environmental factor that increases the likelihood of mutation. (7)
6. Sperm and egg. (7)
8. Short section of DNA on a chromosome. (4)
9. Chemical in chromosomes. (16, 4)
10. Group of similar organisms that produce fertile offspring. (7)
11. Tumours that do not move to other parts of the body. (6)
13. Scientist who introduced the theory of evolution by natural selection. (7, 6)

Down

1. Structure of DNA. (6, 5)
3. Organised picture of an individual's chromosomes. (9)
5. Genetically identical individuals. (6)
7. Scientist who pioneered radiation therapy. (5, 5)
12. Another term for 'characteristic'. (5)

The Diversity of Life

5.1 The Five Kingdoms of Life

1. What is biodiversity?

   _____

   _____

   _____

2. What is classification?

   _____

   _____

   _____

3. Tick the correct column to classify the organisms by kingdom.

	Animal	Plant	Protist	Fungi	Bacteria
Lion					
Elm tree					
Human					
Seaweed					
Lichen					
Bread mould					
Streptococcus					
Goldfish					
Slime mould					
Fly					
Button mushroom					
Lactobacillus					
Cactus					

4. Explain the difference between vertebrate and invertebrate members of the animal kingdom. Give **two** examples of each.

   _____

   _____

   _____

   _____

   _____

   _____

   _____

   _____

5. Insert the following terms into the Venn diagram to compare the characteristics of animals and plants.

Multicellular   Producers   Consumers   Photosynthesis   Respiration   Nucleus

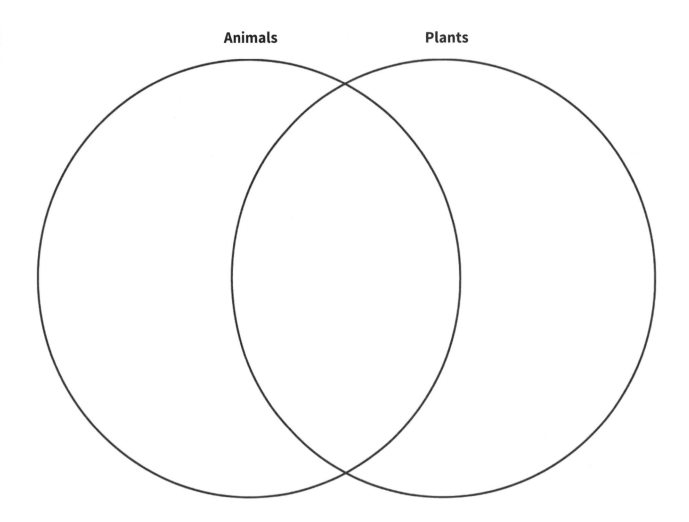

Animals   **Plants**

5.2 Bacteria and Viruses

1. What are microorganisms? Identify **two** different types of microorganism.

   _____

   _____

   _____

2. **a.** What is the term used to describe how bacteria reproduce?

   _____

   b. Calculate how many bacteria would be present in a colony after five generations.

   [ ]

   Answer: _____

3. Explain how bacteria help to recycle nutrients through the Earth's environment.

   _____

   _____

   _____

   _____

4. Give **two** further benefits of bacteria.

   _____

   _____

5. Give **two** negative effects of bacteria.

   _____

   _____

6. Outline **two** ways that we can help slow down the spread of antibiotic resistance in bacteria.

   _____

   _____

   _____

   _____

7. Explain why many scientists do not consider viruses to be living things.

   _____

   _____

   _____

8. What is a vaccine?

   _____

   _____

Crossword

Chapter 5: The Diversity of Life

Across

2. Chemical used to treat diseases caused by microorganisms. (10)
4. First organisms to evolve a nucleus. (8)
5. Small amount of genetic material surrounded by a protein coat. (5)
7. System of naming organisms developed by Carl Linnaeus. (8, 12)
8. Organisms that cause disease. (9)
10. Growth of large numbers of bacteria in a laboratory. (9)
11. Scientist who invented a way to kill pathogens in food and drink. (5, 7)
12. Reproduction in bacteria. (6, 7)

Down

1. Organisms that live off or in another organism. (9)
3. Animals without backbones. (13)
6. Most common organisms on Earth. (8)
9. Changes in an organism's environment. (7)

Chapter 6
The Interactions of Life: Ecology

6.1 The Structure of an Ecosystem

1. What is ecology?

   ecology deals with relations of organisms to one another and to their physical surroundings.

2. List **three** needs that an organism's environment must meet.

   air, food and water.

3. Put the levels of organisation in an ecosystem in order.

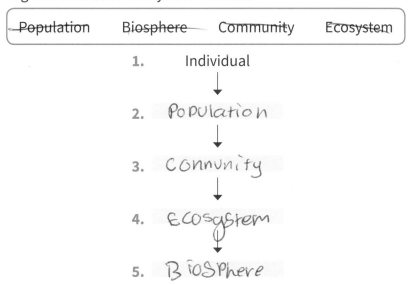

   Population   Biosphere   Community   Ecosystem

   1. Individual
   2. Population
   3. Community
   4. Ecosystem
   5. Biosphere

4. What is a habitat?

   A habitat is a place where an organism makes its home.

5. Explain the difference between the following terms.

   a. Population and community

   A population is a group of the same species living in the same area. A community is a group of different speices living in the same area.

   b. Biome and biosphere

   biome includes living things limited to specific areas on Earth. The Biosphere spans the entire earth and includes all living things on this planet.

6. What is meant by 'the balance of nature'?

   Balance of nature is the fine state of balance in a natural ecosystem due to the effects of the living and non living parts of the environment on each other.

6.2 Interactions of Organisms in an Ecosystem

1. What are abiotic factors? Give **two** examples.

   _____

   _____

   _____

   _____

2. What are biotic factors? Give **two** examples.

   _____

   _____

   _____

   _____

3. Explain how competition between organisms influences the balance of nature.

   _____

   _____

   _____

   _____

   _____

4. Distinguish between predators and prey. Give **one** example of each.

   _____

   _____

   _____

   _____

5. Outline **one** example of a symbiotic relationship between two organisms.

   _____

   _____

   _____

   _____

   _____

6. Outline **one** example of interdependence between two organisms.

   _____

   _____

   _____

   _____

   _____

6.3 Adaptations of Organisms in an Ecosystem

1. What is an adaptation?

   _____

   _____

   _____

2. Outline **two** examples of physical adaptations in organisms.

   _____

   _____

   _____

   _____

   _____

   _____

3. Outline **two** examples of behavioural adaptations in organisms.

   _____

   _____

   _____

   _____

   _____

   _____

4. What does a biologist mean when they refer to 'safety in numbers'?

   _____

   _____

   _____

   _____

   _____

5. What is a niche?

   _____

   _____

   _____

6. Explain why no two organisms can occupy the same niche.

   _____

   _____

   _____

   _____

   _____

   _____

6.4 Feeding Relationships in an Ecosystem

1. What is a feeding relationship?

   _____

   _____

2. Where does the energy entering all food chains come from?

   _____

3. Look at the following food chain.

   | grass ⟶ grasshopper ⟶ mouse ⟶ fox |

   a. Identify the producer: _____

   b. Identify the primary consumer: _____

   c. Identify the secondary consumer: _____

   d. Identify the tertiary consumer: _____

4. Explain the following terms and name **one** organism of each type.

   a. Herbivore: _____

   _____

   b. Carnivore: _____

   _____

   c. Omnivore: _____

   _____

   d. Decomposer:_____

   _____

5. Complete the following sentences using the words below.

   | decomposers   herbivores   predators   omnivores |

   Primary consumers are usually _____ . Secondary consumers are usually _____ .
   Tertiary consumers are the top _____ in an ecosystem.

   In all feeding relationships, dead plant and animal material is broken down by _____ .

6. Distinguish between a food chain and a food web.

   _____

   _____

   _____

7. Explain why the biomass of individual organisms generally increases as you move towards upper levels in a food chain.

   _____

   _____

   _____

6.5 Conducting a Habitat Study

1. With reference to habitat studies, explain the meaning of the saying 'Take only memories, leave only footprints.'

    _____

    _____

2. Name the square frame that is used to survey plants in a habitat.

    _____

3. For what purpose would an ecologist use an identification key?

    _____

    _____

4. Put the steps of a habitat study in the correct order by numbering them 1 to 6.

    Measurement of abiotic (non-living) factors in the habitat. ☐

    Quantitative survey of a species present in the habitat. ☐

    The final report. ☐

    Selection and general description of the habitat. ☐

    Observation of interactions in the habitat. ☐

    Qualitative survey of species in the habitat. ☐

5. Distinguish between a qualitative survey and a quantitative survey of species in a habitat.

    _____

    _____

    _____

6. Suggest a suitable piece of equipment for collecting the following animals.

    a. Spiders: _____

    b. Woodlice: _____

    c. Snails: _____

    d. Butterflies: _____

    e. Fish: _____

7. Name **three** signs of animal activity to look out for when conducting a habitat study.

    _____

    _____

8. Calculate the percentage frequency of ragwort in a field if its presence was noted in three of 25 quadrats that were chosen randomly in a survey of the field.

    ┌───┐
    │   │
    │   │
    │   │
    │   │
    └───┘

    Answer: _____

Crossword

Chapter 6: The Interactions of Life: Ecology

Across

4. Organisms interacting with each other and their environment. (9)
8. Deep sleep over winter to conserve energy. (11)
11. Organism that eats plants and animals. (8)
12. Size of a species' population in an ecosystem. (9)

Down

1. Plant life in an ecosystem. (5)
2. Controls the number of organisms in an ecosystem. (9)
3. Disguise from predators. (10)
5. Relocation during winter in search of better conditions. (9)
6. Non-living factors that affect plants and animals in a habitat. (7)
7. Where an organism lives. (7)
9. Organisms only active at night. (9)
10. Living factors that affect plants and animals in a habitat. (6)

Chapter 7

Structures and Processes of Life: Plants

7.1 The Structure of Flowering Plants

1. List the **four** organs common to all flowering plants.

   _____

   _____

2. Label the diagram showing the basic structure of a flowering plant.

3. What is the role of the bud in a flowering plant?

   _____

   _____

4. Complete the following table to outline **two** functions of the root, stem and leaves of a plant.

Plant organ	Functions
Root	
Stem	
Leaf	

7.2 The Processes of Flowering Plants

1. Outline why plants need water and minerals.

   _____

   _____

   _____

2. Distinguish between the **two** types of transport tissue found in plants.

   _____

   _____

   _____

   _____

   _____

   _____

3. Complete the following sentences using the words below.

leaves	photosynthesis	roots	evaporate
stem	transpiration	soil	xylem

   Water and minerals are taken in from the _____ by the _____. The water and minerals travel up the _____ in the _____ tissue. Water is delivered to the _____ for use in _____.

   Heat energy from the Sun causes water vapour on the surface of the plant to _____. This process is called _____.

4. What do plants use glucose for?

   _____

   _____

5. Explain how plants exchange oxygen and carbon dioxide with the atmosphere. Refer to photosynthesis and respiration in your answer.

   _____

   _____

   _____

   _____

   _____

6. Explain how phototropism helps a plant optimise photosynthesis.

   _____

   _____

   _____

   _____

7.3 Asexual Reproduction in Flowering Plants

1. Identify the **two** forms of reproduction in plants.

   _____

2. Tick the correct column to identify which statements are true and which are false.

	True	False
Only one parent is involved in asexual reproduction		
Gametes are produced during asexual reproduction		
No fertilisation takes place during asexual reproduction		
Asexual reproduction happens naturally		
Asexual reproduction happens artificially		

3. Explain why offspring produced by asexual reproduction are genetically identical to each other and to the parent plant.

   _____

   _____

   _____

   _____

   _____

   _____

4. Outline the role of a runner in the asexual reproduction of a strawberry plant.

   _____

   _____

   _____

   _____

   _____

5. What is vegetative propagation?

   _____

   _____

   _____

6. Suggest a suitable method of vegetative propagation in the following scenarios.

   a. A home gardener wants to grow an identical rosebush to the one he already has.

   _____

   b. A commercial vegetable grower wants to produce a large quantity of disease-free plants.

   _____

   c. A local orchard owner wants to ensure that her apples are consistent in their taste and size each year.

   _____

7.4 Sexual Reproduction in Flowering Plants

1. Name the sex organs in the flower of a plant.

   a. Male: _____

   b. Female: _____

2. Label the diagram showing the structure of a flower.

   _____ _____   _____

   _____ _____

   _____   _____

   _____ _____   _____

   _____ _____

3. Put the stages of sexual reproduction of a flowering plant in the correct order by numbering them 1 to 5.

   Seed (and fruit) formation   ☐

   Germination   ☐

   Pollination   ☐

   Seed (and fruit) dispersal   ☐

   Fertilisation   ☐

4. Explain why seeds and fruits are dispersed away from the parent plant before germination.

   _____

   _____

   _____

   _____

5. Name **two** types of seed (and fruit) dispersal.

   _____

   _____

6. Identify the **three** environmental factors that must be suitable before a seed can germinate.

   _____

   _____

   _____

7. Insert the following terms into the Venn diagram to compare the characteristics of asexual reproduction and sexual reproduction in flowering plants.

One parent	Two parents	Flower	Identical offspring
Non-identical offspring		Gametes	Fertilisation
	Happens naturally	Happens artificially	

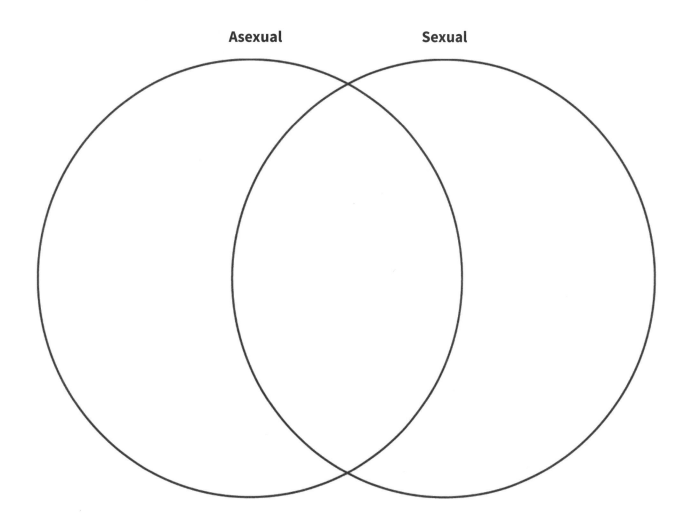

Asexual   **Sexual**

Crossword

Chapter 7: Structures and Processes of Life: Plants

Across

6. Short stem with fleshy leaves and buds. (4)
7. Part of stamen that produces pollen and sperm. (6)
9. Growth of seed to form a new plant. (11)
11. Process by which a plant makes its own food. (14)
13. Growth of a plant in response to gravity. (10)
14. Plant tissue visible on a leaf blade or celery stem. (8, 6)

Down

1. Reproduction of plants from a cultured tissue sample. (16)
2. Tissue that transports food around a plant. (6)
3. Transfer of pollen from stamen to carpel. (11)
4. Part of carpel that produces the egg. (5)
5. Part of carpel that acts as landing area for pollen. (6)
8. Loss of water vapour from leaf surface. (13)
10. Part of a plant that supports buds, leaves and flowers. (4)
12. Part of a plant that grows above ground. (5)

Chapter 8

Structures and Processes of Life: Humans

8.1 The Organisation of Humans

1. What is specialisation?

   _____

   _____

2. What is division of labour?

   _____

   _____

3. What is a system?

   _____

4. Name the level of organisation above a system.

   _____

5. Match each human system to its function.

System		Function	
1.	Immune	a.	Breaks down food
2.	Nervous	b.	Removes waste
3.	Reproductive	c.	Allows the body to move
4.	Digestive	d.	Controls body functions
5.	Circulatory	e.	Protects against disease
6.	Respiratory	f.	Produces hormones
7.	Musculoskeletal	g.	Transports nutrients
8.	Excretory	h.	Exchanges gases
9.	Endocrine	i.	Produces offspring

1.	2.	3.	4.	5.	6.	7.	8.	9.

8.2 The Digestive System

1. Describe the **two** types of digestion.

   a. Physical digestion: _____

   _____

   b. Chemical digestion: _____

   _____

2. Put the stages of human nutrition in the correct order by numbering them 1 to 5.

   Assimilation   ☐

   Absorption   ☐

   Egestion   ☐

   Digestion   ☐

   Ingestion   ☐

3. Explain the difference between absorption and assimilation.

   _____

   _____

   _____

   _____

4. Label the parts of the digestive system.

5. Outline the role of the stomach in digestion.

   _____

   _____

   _____

6. List the **four** different types of teeth.

   _____   _____

   _____   _____

8.3 The Circulatory System

1. List the **three** main roles of the circulatory system.

   _____

   _____

   _____

2. Complete the following sentences using the words below.

   > white   clot   heat   disease   red
   >
   > fragments   plasma   haemoglobin

   There are three types of blood cell. Oxygen is transported by the _____ blood cells, which contain _____ .

   The main function of _____ blood cells is to protect the body from _____ .

   Platelets are _____ of cells that help the blood to _____ . _____ transports the blood cells around the body, along with dissolved substances and _____ .

3. Complete the table to outline **two** features of each of the different types of blood vessels.

Blood vessel	Features
Arteries	
Veins	
Capillaries	

4. Put the stages of the cycle of blood through the body (beginning at the right atrium of the heart) in the correct order by numbering them 1 to 8.

   Blood is forced through a semilunar valve into the pulmonary artery ☐

   Blood is deoxygenated as it travels through capillaries, veins and venae cavae, back to the right atrium ☐

   Blood is delivered to the lungs, where it is oxygenated ☐

   Blood is forced through a semilunar valve into the aorta ☐

   Oxygenated blood is delivered to the left atrium by the pulmonary vein ☐

   Blood is pumped through a cuspid valve into the left ventricle ☐

   Deoxygenated blood enters the right atrium of the heart ☐

   Blood is pumped through a cuspid valve into the right ventricle ☐

8.4 The Respiratory System

1. List the **three** main roles of the respiratory system.

    _____

    _____

    _____

2. Label the parts of the respiratory system.

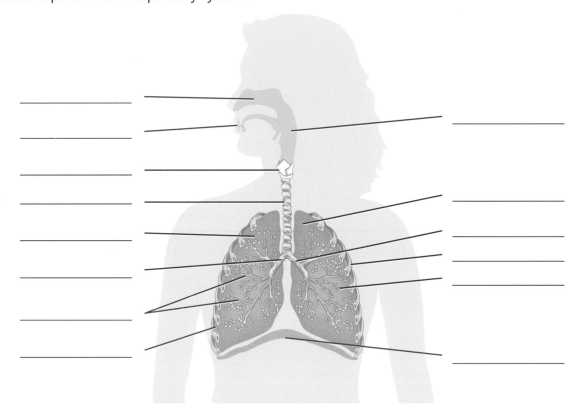

3. Match each part of the respiratory system with a function it carries out.

Part of respiratory system		Function	
1.	Mouth and nose	a.	Allow air to flow into and out of lungs
2.	Trachea	b.	Opening for respiratory and digestive systems
3.	Larynx	c.	Supply oxygen to cells
4.	Bronchus	d.	Protects the heart and lungs
5.	Pharynx	e.	Remove dust and microorganisms
6.	Intercostal muscles	f.	Contracts and expands to move air in and out of the lungs
7.	Ribs	g.	Moves the ribs
8.	Lungs	h.	Plays a role in speech
9.	Diaphragm	i.	Allows air to flow from the pharynx to the bronchus

1.	2.	3.	4.	5.	6.	7.	8.	9.

4. Outline **two** ways alveoli are adapted for the exchange of gases.

_____

_____

_____

_____

_____

_____

5. Complete the following sentences using the words below.

| in   expand   increases   decreases   contract   out |

During inhalation, the lungs _____ and the air pressure within them _____ . Air is drawn _____ from the atmosphere.

During exhalation, the lungs _____ and the air pressure in the lungs _____ . Air is pushed _____ to the atmosphere.

8.5 The Reproductive System

1. What is puberty?

   _____

   _____

   _____

2. **a.** Identify **two** physical changes that take place in females during puberty.

   _____

   _____

   b. Identify **two** physical changes that take place in males during puberty.

   _____

   _____

3. Label the parts of the female reproductive system.

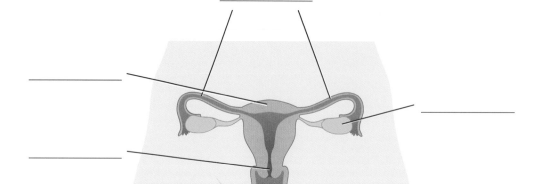

4. Outline the function of the ovaries.

   _____

   _____

5. Put the stages of the menstrual cycle in the correct order by numbering them 1 to 5.

   Lining of the womb begins to break down again if no embryo is implanted ☐

   Lining of the womb detaches and discharges through the vagina ☐

   Lining of the womb continues to build up in anticipation of embryo implantation ☐

   Egg is released from the ovary and enters the fallopian tube ☐

   Lining of the womb is built up with blood vessels ☐

6. Label the parts of the male reproductive system.

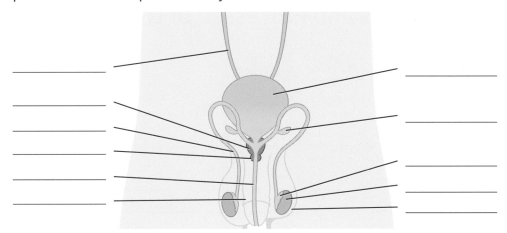

7. Outline the function of the testes.

_____

_____

8. Distinguish between fertilisation and implantation.

_____

_____

_____

_____

9. Identify **two** functions of the placenta.

_____

_____

_____

10. What is the function of the amniotic sac?

_____

_____

_____

11. List the **three** stages of birth.

_____

_____

_____

12. Complete the following table by giving **one** example of each type of contraception.

Method	Example
Natural	
Mechanical	
Chemical	
Surgical	

Crossword

Chapter 8: Structures and Processes of Life: Humans

Across

2. Liquid part of blood. (6)
3. Primary sexual organ in males. (6)
4. Separates the two sides of the heart. (6)
7. Expandable bag that churns and stores food. (7)
9. Where fertilisation usually takes place. (9, 5)
10. Largest internal organ. (5)
12. Tiny air sacs in the lungs. (8)
13. Throat. (7)
14. Narrow entrance to the uterus. (6)
15. Pigment in red blood cells. (11)
16. Release of undigested food through the anus. (8)

Down

1. Production of breast milk. (9)
5. Teeth that crush and grind food. (6)
6. Wave of vibration travelling through the wall of an artery. (5)
8. Food pipe. (10)
11. Line the small intestine to increase surface area. (5)

Chemical World

What Matter is Made Of

9.1 The Particle Theory and States of Matter

1. What is matter?

   _____

   _____

2. Name the **three** states of matter.

   _____

   _____

   _____

3. Outline the particle theory.

   _____

   _____

   _____

   _____

   _____

4. In the boxes below, draw the arrangement of particles in a solid, a liquid and a gas.

Solid	Liquid	Gas

5. Complete the following table to show the properties of solids, liquids and gases.

Solids	Liquids	Gases
Fixed mass		
	Fixed volume	
		No fixed shape
Does not flow		
	Cannot be compressed	

6. Explain why gases can be compressed and solids and liquids cannot.

_____

_____

_____

_____

7. Outline how you would show that:

   a. air has mass: _____

   _____

   _____

   _____

   b. air takes up space: _____

   _____

   _____

   _____

9.2 Diffusion

1. What is diffusion?

_____

_____

2. Dave carried out an investigation to find out how the concentration of a substance affects the rate of diffusion. He spaced squares of litmus paper at 3 cm intervals inside a glass tube. He added 1 drop of ammonia solution to a piece of cotton wool and put it at the end of the tube. He then timed how long it took each litmus paper to change colour. He repeated this process again, this time using 5 drops of ammonia.

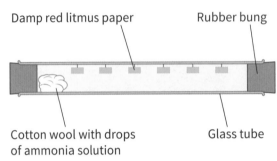

Damp red litmus paper   Rubber bung

Cotton wool with drops
of ammonia solution   Glass tube

The results of Dave's investigation are shown in the table below.

No. of drops of ammonia	3 cm	6 cm	9 cm	12 cm	15 cm
1	6 seconds	13 seconds	18 seconds	24 seconds	31 seconds
5	2 seconds	6 seconds	11 seconds	14 seconds	20 seconds

a. Draw a graph of distance versus time for the two concentrations of ammonia solution. (Show distance on the *x*-axis.)

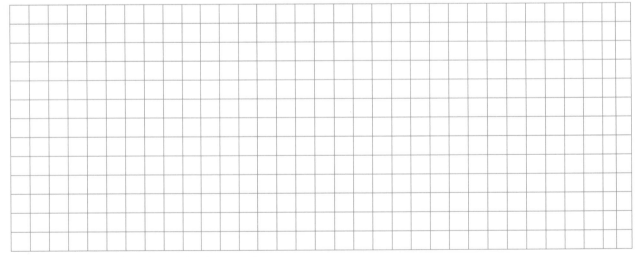

b. Describe the results shown in the graph.

_____

_____

_____

_____

9.3 Changes of State

1. Identify the changes of state shown in the following diagram.

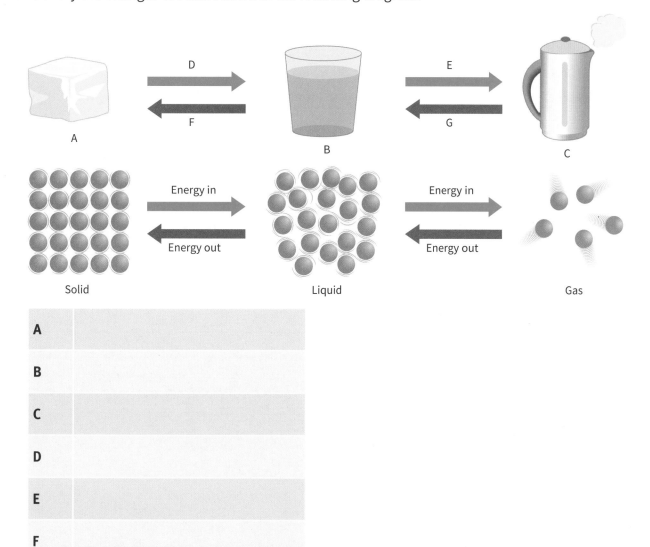

A	
B	
C	
D	
E	
F	
G	

2. Complete the following sentences using the words below.

> gain　freezing　boiling　lose　melting

When a solid is heated, the particles _____ energy and the solid becomes a liquid.
This is called _____ .

When a liquid is heated, the particles break free from each other and the liquid becomes a gas.
This is called _____ .

When a liquid is cooled, the particles _____ energy and the liquid becomes a solid.
This is called _____ .

3. Name the state of matter that forms when a:

   a. solid melts: _____

   b. liquid evaporates: _____

   c. gas condenses: _____

   d. solid sublimes: _____

   e. liquid freezes: _____

4. Water droplets form on the outside of a glass that contains a cold drink. Explain why this happens.

   _____

   _____

   _____

   _____

5. Explain what is meant by the term **sublimation** and give **one** example.

   _____

   _____

   _____

   _____

   _____

9.4 Properties of Materials

1. A material is described as being flexible, transparent and strong. Explain these terms.

   a. Flexible: _____

   b. Transparent: _____

   c. Strong: _____

2. Complete the following table to show **two** properties each item must have.

Item	Properties
Raincoat	
Window	
Sweeping brush	
Trampoline	
Fruit bowl	

3. Put the steps of the product life cycle in the correct order by numbering them 1 to 5.

   Packaging and distribution ☐

   Product use ☐

   End-of-life disposal ☐

   Manufacturing ☐

   Extraction of raw materials ☐

4. Outline **two** advantages of recycling.

   _____

   _____

5. What is meant by the term **carbon footprint**?

   _____

   _____

   _____

9.5 Physical Change Versus Chemical Change

1. Explain the difference between a chemical change and a physical change.

   _____

   _____

   _____

   _____

2. Outline the law of conservation of mass.

   _____

   _____

   _____

3. Tick the correct column to identify the type of change being described.

	Physical change	Chemical change
Burning magnesium ribbon		
Using sand paper to smooth down a surface		
Getting a hair cut		
Milk turning sour		
Melting chocolate		
Chopping wood		
Squeezing an orange		
Blowing up a balloon		
Switching on a torch		
A candle burning		
A candle melting		

4. Jane set up the following investigation.

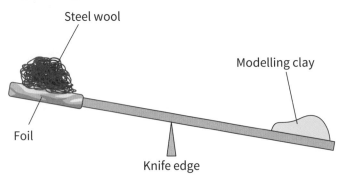

a. When the steel wool was burned with a Bunsen burner flame, the following happened. Explain why.

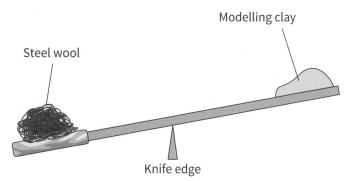

Modelling clay

Steel wool

Knife edge

_____

_____

_____

_____

_____

b. Does this investigation obey the law of conservation of matter? Explain your answer.

_____

_____

_____

_____

_____

_____

Crossword

Chapter 9: What Matter is Made Of

Across

2. Space taken up by a substance. (6)
4. Opposite of waterproof. (9)
7. Temperature at which a substance boils. (7, 5)
8. Change in which a new substance is formed. (8)
9. Change of a solid to a gas without going through the liquid state. (11)
10. Change in which no new substance is formed. (8)
11. Can be carried out on gases but not solids or liquids. (11)
12. Change of state from a liquid to a solid. (8)
13. Reuse of materials. (9)

Down

1. Theory describing the properties of matter. (8, 6)
3. Takes up space and has a mass. (6)
5. Any substance released into the atmosphere. (8)
6. Spreading out of a gas to fill space. (9)

Chapter 10

The Building Blocks of the Chemical World

10.1 Atoms and Elements

1. What is an atom?

   _____

2. What is an element?

   _____

3. John Dalton carried out investigations into the existence of atoms. What suggestions did he make?

   _____

   _____

   _____

   _____

4. Suggest a reason why scientists use chemical symbols for elements.

   _____

   _____

5. Match the element with its chemical symbol.

Element		Chemical symbol	
1.	Chlorine	a.	K
2.	Neon	b.	Na
3.	Sulfur	c.	H
4.	Sodium	d.	Ne
5.	Carbon	e.	S
6.	Potassium	f.	N
7.	Nitrogen	g.	Cl
8.	Hydrogen	h.	C

1.	2.	3.	4.	5.	6.	7.	8.

6. Name **one** element that is:

   a. Solid at room temperature: _____

   b. Liquid at room temperature: _____

   c. Gas at room temperature: _____

10.2 Subatomic Particles

1. Complete the table below to describe each subatomic particle.

	Proton	Neutron	Electron
Location in the atom			
Charge			
Mass			

2. What is meant by the atomic number of an atom?

_____

_____

_____

3. What is atomic mass?

_____

_____

_____

4. Explain why the electrons in an atom are not included when working out atomic mass.

_____

_____

_____

5. The atoms of an element contain 33 protons and 42 neutrons. Identify:

   a. The name of the element: _____

   b. The chemical symbol for the element: _____

   c. The mass number of the element: _____

   d. The number of electrons in a neutral atom of the element: _____

6. Use the periodic table on page 462 of your *Catalyst* textbook to complete the following table.

Atomic number	Mass number	Number of protons	Number of neutrons	Number of electrons	Name of element	Symbol of element
						Mg
				14		
					Lithium	
19						
	45					

10.3 Atomic Structure

1. What does the electronic configuration of an atom describe?

_____

_____

2. Draw a Bohr model and write the electronic configuration of the following atoms.

Hydrogen	**Magnesium**
H: _____	Mg: _____
Neon	**Phosphorus**
Ne: _____	P: _____

3. Using your knowledge of isotopes, answer the following questions about the isotopes of Boron (Boron–10 and Boron–11).

   a. What is the atomic number of Boron? _____

   b. How many protons, neutrons and electrons does isotope B-10 have? _____

   _____

   c. How many protons, neutrons and electrons does isotope B-11 have? _____

   _____

   d. What do the isotopes have in common? _____

   _____

   e. How do the isotopes differ? _____

   _____

10.4 The Periodic Table of the Elements

1. Name **two** items of information that can be found in the periodic table.

_____

_____

2. Match the scientist with their contribution to the development of the periodic table.

Scientist		Contribution	
1.	Johann Döbereiner	a.	Organised elements with similar properties into a table of periodic patterns, leaving gaps for as yet undiscovered elements
2.	John Newland	b.	Organised elements into subgroups based on their similarities
3.	Dmitri Mendeleev	c.	Organised the elements in order of the mass of the atoms of each element and discovered that the every eighth element in the first fifteen shared properties

1.	2.	3.

3. Outline the difference between groups and periods on the periodic table.

_____

_____

_____

4. What do elements in the same group have in common with each other?

_____

_____

5. Outline how are elements are arranged in the modern periodic table.

_____

_____

6. Complete the table by using the period and group number provided to locate elements and their symbols on the periodic table.

Period number	Group number	Element	Symbol
3	1	Sodium	Na
4	3		
2	4		
4	7		
1	8		
3	3		

7. Explain why carbon dioxide (CO_2) does not appear on the periodic table.

_____

_____

10.5 Metals and Non-Metals

1. Explain the following terms.

   a. Malleable: _____

   _____

   b. Ductile: _____

   _____

   c. Conductor: _____

   _____

   d. Insulator: _____

   _____

2. Tick the correct column to identify the following elements as metals or non-metals.

Element	Metal	Non-metal
Carbon		
Sodium		
Beryllium		
Sulfur		
Neon		
Potassium		
Calcium		
Chlorine		
Argon		

3. What is an alloy?

   _____

   _____

4. Give **two** examples of alloys and name the elements they are composed of.

   _____

   _____

5. Give **one** advantage of an alloy versus a metal it its pure state.

   _____

   _____

Crossword

Chapter 10: The Building Blocks of the Chemical World

Across

3. Nobel gases group number. (5)
9. Describes the arrangement of electrons in an atom. (10, 13)
12. Au. (4)

Down

1. Scientist who developed a model for atomic structure. (5, 4)
2. Same atomic number but different mass number. (7)
3. Substance made of only one type of atom. (7)
4. Group 7 elements. (8)
5. Orbits the nucleus. (8)
6. Rows in the periodic table. (7)
7. Positive particle. (6)
8. Number of electrons that fit in the first electron shell. (3)
10. Centre of an atom. (7)
11. Columns in the periodic table. (6)

Chapter 11

Compounds, Mixtures and Solutions

11.1 Compounds and Mixtures

1. What is a compound? Give **one** example.

   _____

   _____

   _____

2. What is a mixture? Give **one** example.

   _____

   _____

   _____

3. Complete the table by placing the following substances in the correct columns.

   > gold ring   blood   air   carbon dioxide   ice   steam
   > copper wire   aluminium foil   sea water   coffee   helium
   > diamond   tears   milk   sugar

Elements	Compounds	Mixtures

4. Explain why sodium chloride (table salt) does not react in your mouth but sodium metal is very reactive with water.

   _____

   _____

   _____

   _____

5. Look at the following model and answer the complete the table.

A

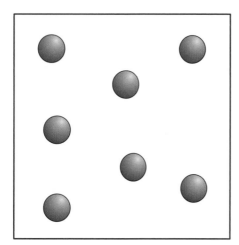

B

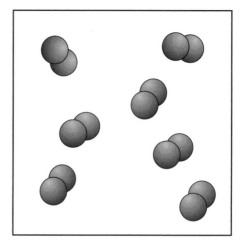

C

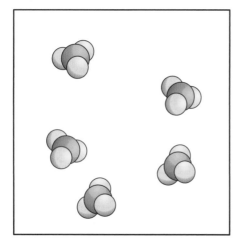

D

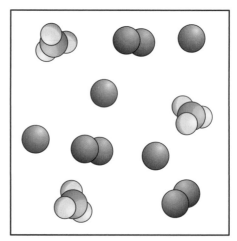

	Shown in box letter(s)
A representation of an element	
A representation of a mixture	
A representation of a compound	
A representation of a pure substance	
A representation of an impure substance	
A representation of a substance made up of atoms	
A representation of a substance made up of molecules	

11.2 Solutions

1. What is a solution?

   _____

2. Water is described as the universal solvent.

   a. What is a solvent?

   _____

   _____

   b. Name **one** substance that dissolves in water.

   _____

   c. Name **one** substance that does not dissolve in water.

   _____

3. Is dissolving a physical change or a chemical change? Explain your answer.

   _____

   _____

   _____

4. Define the term **solubility**.

   _____

   _____

5. Identify the **three** factors that affect the solubility of a substance.

   _____

   _____

   _____

6. Draw a simple graph to show the solubility curve you would expect to see in a solution in which a solid solute is dissolved at increasing temperatures.

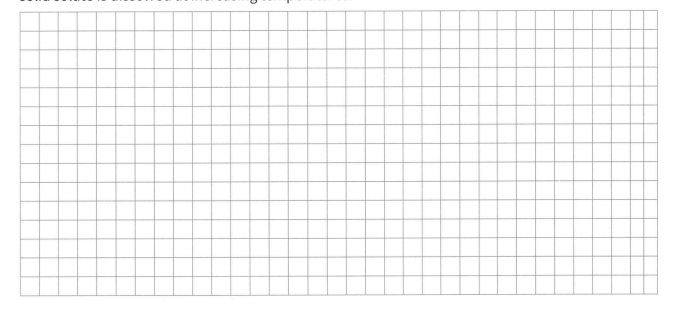

11.3 Crystallisation

1. Draw diagrams to show the particles of a solute in a dilute solution, a concentrated solution and a saturated solution.

Dilute solution	Concentrated solution	Saturated solution

2. Outline **two** ways that a dilute solution can be made more concentrated.

_____

_____

_____

3. Outline **one** way that a concentrated solution can be made more dilute.

_____

_____

4. Use the data in the table below to calculate the mass of crystals that will form when a saturated solution of potassium bromide containing 100 g of water at 80 °C is cooled to 40 °C.

Temperature (°C)	20	40	60	80	100
Solubility g/100 g	65	76	86	95	104

Answer: _____

5. Use the data in the table below to calculate the mass of crystals that will form when a saturated solution of copper sulfate containing 100 g of water at 100 °C is cooled to 10 °C.

Temperature (°C)	0	10	40	80	100
Solubility g/100 g	14	17	29	55	75

Answer: _____

6. Explain how the solubility of a gas dissolved in a liquid is affected by temperature.

_____

_____

_____

11.4 Separating Mixtures

1. Complete the following table by suggesting a method for separating each mixture and naming the piece of equipment you would need to carry out the separation.

Mixture	Separation technique	Equipment needed
Sand and iron filings		
Salt and sand		
Alcohol and water		
Salt and water		
Coloured inks in a pen		
Sand, salt and iron filings		
Water and oil		

2. Explain why a mixture of water and alcohol can be separated by distillation.

_____

_____

_____

_____

3. Complete the following table by naming **two** everyday plastics, their properties and an example of a product that is made of each plastic.

Plastic	Properties	Product

4. What does it mean if a substance is described as 'biodegradable'?

_____

_____

5. **a.** Outline **one** advantage of fracking.

_____

_____

b. Outline **one** disadvantage of fracking.

_____

_____

Crossword

Chapter 11: Compounds, Mixtures and Solutions

Across

4. Controversial method of natural gas extraction. (8)
6. Solution in which no more solute can be dissolved. (9)
8. Mixture of a solute and a solvent. (8)
10. Gas dissolved in fizzy drinks. (6, 7)
11. Technique used to separate food colouring mixture. (14)

Down

1. Form after the cooling of a saturated solution. (8)
2. Chemical name for table salt. (6, 8)
3. Technique used to separate sand and water. (10)
5. Substance that does not dissolve in a solvent. (9)
7. Condenser used in distillation. (7)
9. Smallest unit of a plastic. (7)

Chapter 12

Chemical Reactions: Fast and Slow

12.1 Chemical Reactions

1. What is a reactant?

   _____

2. What is a product?

   _____

3. Complete the following table to show the reactants needed to form each product.

Product (chemical formula)	Reactants
Table salt (NaCl)	
Carbon dioxide (CO_2)	
Water (H_2O)	
Glucose ($C_6H_{12}O_6$)	
Methane CH_4	
Copper sulfate ($CuSO_4$)	
Sodium carbonate (Na_2CO_3)	

4. Identify **three** everyday examples of chemical reactions.

   _____

   _____

5. Explain, in terms of energy, what happens to chemical bonds during a chemical reaction.

   _____

   _____

   _____

6. Identify **four** observations that might be made during a chemical reaction.

   _____

   _____

   _____

7. Explain what is meant by the term **effervescence**.

   _____

   _____

12.2 Endothermic and Exothermic Reactions

1. Outline the difference between an endothermic reaction and an exothermic reaction.

   _____

   _____

2. Complete the table to show the reactions as either endothermic or exothermic. Explain your choice.

Reaction	Endothermic or exothermic?	Explanation
Ice melts to form water		
Steam condenses to form water		
Solid iodine sublimes to form gaseous iodine		
Cold pack used in a football match to treat an injury		
Plant producing food by photosynthesis		
Getting energy from food (respiration)		
Firework exploding		

3. Outline what you would observe if you used a thermometer in an exothermic reaction.

   _____

   _____

   _____

4. What is an energy profile diagram?

_____

_____

5. Draw an energy profile diagram to show an endothermic reaction.

6. Draw an energy profile diagram to show an exothermic reaction.

12.3 How Do Chemical Reactions Happen?

1. What is the collision theory?

_____

_____

_____

2. Look at the diagram below and answer the questions that follow.

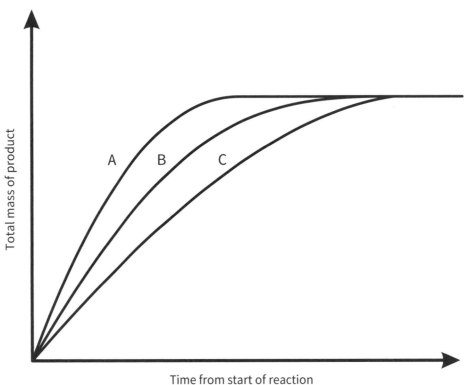

a. Which line shows the greatest rate? _____

b. Which line shows the lowest rate? _____

3. Explain why the rate of a reaction generally decreases over time.

_____

_____

_____

4. Outline **two** ways in which the rate of a reaction can be monitored.

_____

_____

_____

_____

_____

5. Draw a rate of reaction graph for the data in the following table.

Time (min)	Volume of gas produced (cm³)
0	0
1	34
2	42
3	48
4	50
5	50

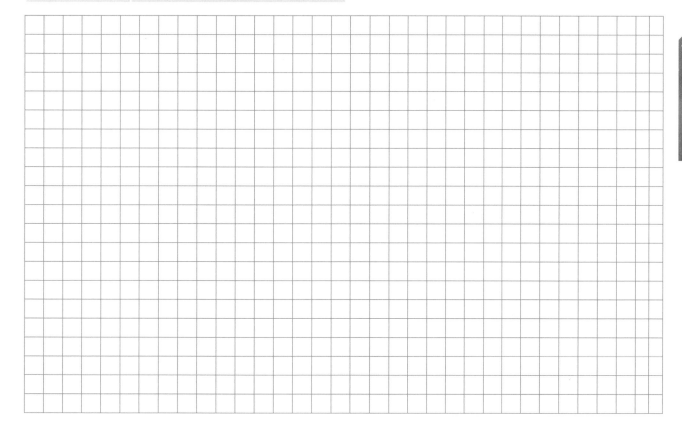

12.4 Factors Affecting the Rate of a Reaction

1. Identify the **four** factors that influence the rate of a chemical reaction.

   _____

   _____

   _____

   _____

2. Explain why diced potatoes cook quicker than whole potatoes.

   _____

   _____

   _____

   _____

3. Explain why food is stored in the fridge to prevent it from going off.

   _____

   _____

   _____

   _____

4. What is a catalyst?

   _____

   _____

5. Draw an energy profile diagram for an exothermic reaction to show how a catalyst lowers the activation energy of a reaction.

12.5 Production of Gases

1. Complete the table below to show the reactants and method of collection in the production of oxygen and carbon dioxide gases.

Gas	Reactants	Method of collection
Oxygen		
Carbon dioxide		

2. In the production of oxygen gas, explain why the gas can be collected by the displacement of water from a gas jar.

_____

_____

_____

3. In the production of carbon dioxide gas, explain why the gas can be collected by the downward displacement of air from a gas jar.

_____

_____

_____

4. Outline a chemical test for oxygen gas.

_____

_____

_____

5. Outline a chemical test for carbon dioxide gas.

_____

_____

_____

6. Describe how the rate of reaction could be increased in the production of:

   a. oxygen gas: _____

   _____

   b. carbon dioxide gas: _____

   _____

7. Give **one** use of:

   a. oxygen gas: _____

   _____

   b. carbon dioxide gas: _____

   _____

Crossword

Chapter 12: Chemical Reactions: Fast and Slow

Across

3. Factor that influences the rate of a reaction. (11)
4. Type of chemical reaction when ice changes to water. (11)
6. Chemical reaction that releases heat. (10)
10. Production of gas bubbles. (13)
11. Theory describing how particles collide in a chemical reaction. (9, 6)
12. Substance that speeds up the rate of a chemical reaction. (8)
13. Minimum energy required for a reaction to happen. (10, 6)

Down

1. Marble chips. (7, 9)
2. Chemical used to test for carbon dioxide. (9)
5. Gas produced when hydrogen decomposes. (6)
7. New substance formed in a chemical reaction. (7)
8. Reactant needed to make water. (8)
9. Chemical that reacts in a chemical reaction. (8)

Chapter 13

Acids and Bases

13.1 Acids and Bases

1. **a.** Identify **two** everyday acids.

   _____

   b. Identify **two** laboratory acids.

   _____

2. **a.** Identify **two** everyday bases.

   _____

   b. Identify **two** laboratory bases.

   _____

3. Many acids and bases are described as **corrosive**. Explain what this means.

   _____

   _____

   _____

4. Outline the safety precautions that should be taken when handling laboratory acids and bases.

   _____

   _____

   _____

   _____

5. Describe the difference between a dilute acid and concentrated acid.

   _____

   _____

   _____

   _____

6. What is meant by the term **alkali**?

   _____

   _____

   _____

7. What is meant by the term **neutral substance**?

   _____

   _____

   _____

13.2 pH and Indicators

1. Why do scientists use the pH scale?

   _____

   _____

2. Complete the following sentences using the words below.

   | acidic   alkaline   neutral |

   The pH scale goes from 0 to 14. A substance that has a pH of 7 on the pH scale is
   _____ . A substance that has a pH below 7 is _____ . A substance that
   has a pH above 7 is _____ .

3. What is an indicator?

   _____

   _____

   _____

4. Complete the following table to show the effect of an acid and base on litmus indicator.

	Litmus colour
Acid	
Base	

5. State **one** advantage of universal indicator over litmus indicator.

   _____

   _____

6. Name **two** natural substances from which acid/base indicators can be extracted.

   _____

   _____

7. Oranges and lemons both contain citric acid. The pH of lemons is approximately 2 and the pH of
   oranges is approximately 3.5. Explain the difference in the pH of lemons and oranges.

   _____

   _____

   _____

   _____

   _____

13.3 Neutralisation

85

1. What name is given to reaction between acids and bases?
   _____

2. Describe **one** everyday example of a neutralisation reaction.
   _____
   _____
   _____

3. What is a titration?
   _____
   _____

4. Complete the following table to show how equipment is used in a titration.

Equipment	How the equipment is used
Burette	
Pipette	
Conical	

5. Write a word equation for the following reactions.
   a. Acid and base: _____
   _____
   b. Acid and carbonate: _____
   _____
   c. Acid and metal: _____
   _____

6. Outline a test for the presence of hydrogen gas.
   _____
   _____

7. Suggest a cure for a bee sting and explain your choice.
   _____
   _____

8. Suggest a cure for a wasp sting and explain your choice.
   _____
   _____

Crossword

Chapter 13: Acids and Bases

Across

2. Gas formed when an acid and a metal react. (8)
3. Technique to find out how much acid is needed to neutralise an alkali. (9)
5. Acid used to flavour chips. (8)
6. Measures how acidic or basic a substance is. (2, 5)
7. Location of hydrochloric acid in the body. (7)
8. Chemical that changes colour to show if a substance is acidic or basic. (9)
9. Base that can dissolve in water. (6)
11. Gas formed when an acid and carbonate react. (6, 7)

Down

1. Reaction between an acid and a base. (14)
4. Substance that is not an acid or a base. (7)
10. Turns blue litmus red. (4)

Chapter 14

Chemical Reactions: Bonding

14.1 Types of Chemical Reactions

1. Match the chemical reaction with its description.

Chemical reaction		Description	
1.	Oxidation	a.	Reactions between an acid and a base to form a salt and water
2.	Decomposition	b.	Reaction that is produced by electricity or produces electricity
3.	Neutralisation	c.	Reaction that involves breaking down a substance into simpler compounds or elements
4.	Electrolysis	d.	Reaction when a substance reacts with oxygen

1.	2.	3.	4.

2. What is a hydrocarbon?

3. Explain how the law of conservation of mass applies to chemical reactions.

4. Write a word equation to describe what happens when copper is burned in oxygen.

5. Identify the **three** factors necessary for a fire to start.

6. What form of energy is produced when a fuel burns?

7. Outline **one** method for putting out a fire. Explain why it works.

8. Explain how a household can prevent carbon monoxide poisoning.

14.2 Reactions of Metals

1. Explain why group 2 metals are called the alkaline earth metals.

   _____

   _____

   _____

2. Write a word equation for the following reactions.

   a. Alkali metal and water

   _____

   b. Alkaline earth metal and oxygen

   _____

3. Identify **two** everyday uses of alkali metals.

   _____

   _____

4. What is meant by the term **corrosion**?

   _____

   _____

5. Outline **two** methods that can be used to prevent the corrosion of metals.

   _____

   _____

   _____

   _____

   _____

   _____

6. Put the metals in order of reactivity (starting with the least reactive) by numbering them 1 to 5.

   Magnesium ☐

   Copper ☐

   Calcium ☐

   Zinc ☐

   Gold ☐

14.3 Atoms in Reactions

1. Table salt (NaCl) and water (H_2O) are both compounds. Table salt is a compound with ionic bonds and water is a compound with covalent bonds. Explain the difference between ionic and covalent bonds.

   _____

   _____

   _____

   _____

   _____

2. Explain how a negative ion forms.

   _____

   _____

   _____

3. Explain how a positive ion forms.

   _____

   _____

   _____

   _____

4. Complete the following table to show the ion formed by each element:

Element	Ion formed
Sodium	
Calcium	
Aluminium	
Iodine	
Fluorine	
Oxygen	
Lithium	

5. What properties of a material does the bond type determine?

_____

_____

_____

_____

6. Tick the correct column to identify the properties of ionic substances and covalent substances.

	Ionic substances	Covalent substances
Usually liquids or gases		
Conduct electricity in liquid form or if they dissolve in water		
Have low melting points and boiling points		
Do not conduct electricity		
Usually solids		
High melting points and boiling points		

7. Using atomic structure and your knowledge of bonding, explain why noble gases are so unreactive.

_____

_____

_____

_____

_____

14.4 Chemical Formulae

1. Using the terms **coefficient** and **subscript**, explain the difference between the numbers in the chemical formula $2H_2O$.

   _____

   _____

   _____

2. Complete the following table to show the ratio of each element present in the named compound.

Name of compound	Chemical formula	Elements present	Ratio of elements present
Lithium chloride	LiCl	Lithium Chlorine	Li : Cl 1 : 1
Magnesium sulfide	MgS		
Dihydrogen monoxide	H_2O		
Glucose	$C_6H_{12}O_6$		
Carbon monoxide	CO		

3. Use the periodic table to write the chemical formulae for the following ionic compounds.

Ionic compound	Ion 1	Ion 2	Chemical formula
Lithium chloride	Li^{+1}	Cl^{-1}	LiCl
Calcium oxide			
Magnesium fluoride			
Lithium oxide			
Barium oxide			

4. What is meant by the term **valency**?

   _____

   _____

   _____

5. Use the periodic table to write the chemical formulae for the following covalent compounds.

Covalent compound	Valency element 1	Valency element 2	Chemical formula
Dihydrogen sulfide	H = 1	S = 2	H_2S
Carbon dioxide			
Carbon monoxide			

Crossword

Chapter 14: Chemical Reactions: Bonding

Across

3. Formed when an atom loses or gains an electron. (3)
4. Colour of copper oxide. (5)
6. Chemical reaction produced by electricity. (12)
9. Dihydrogen monoxide. (5)
12. Substance that burns in oxygen to produce heat energy. (4)

Down

1. Combining power of an element. (7)
2. Bond formed when elements share electrons. (8)
5. Most reactive metal. (9)
7. Gas that makes up approximately 20 per cent of air. (6)
8. Type of bonding in table salt. (5)
10. Soft metals with low melting points. (6)
11. Common name for iron oxide. (4)

Physical World

Chapter 15

Measuring the Physical World

15.1 SI Units

1. What is a physical quantity?

   _____

2. Explain why is it important to have a universal system of measurement.

   _____

   _____

   _____

3. Complete the following table.

Physical quantity	Symbol	SI unit of measurement (and symbol)
	t	
Electric current		
Length		
	T	
		kilogram (kg)

4. State the formulae used to calculate the following derived units.

   For example:

   $$\text{Density (kg/m}^3) = \frac{\text{Mass (kg)}}{\text{Volume (m}^3)}$$

   a. Speed (m/s)

   b. Power (W)

   c. Voltage (V)

15.2 Measuring Length and Area

1. What is the SI unit for length?

_____

2. Suggest a suitable instrument for measuring the following objects.

   a. The diameter of a screw: _____

   b. The length and width of a rectangular textbook: _____

   c. The thickness of a coin: _____

   d. The distance between two points on a map: _____

   e. The length of a football field: _____

   f. The height of a school desk: _____

3. What is area?

   _____

   _____

4. Explain why the unit for area is always squared.

   _____

   _____

5. Calculate the area of the following objects.

   a.   **b.**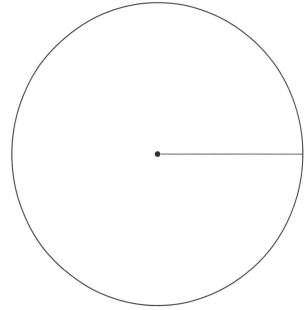

6. Outline a method for estimating the area of your school tie.

   _____

   _____

   _____

   _____

   _____

15.3 Measuring Mass and Volume

1. What is mass?

   _____

2. Suggest a suitable instrument for measuring the mass of the following objects.

   a. A person: _____

   b. A beaker of liquid: _____

   c. An apple: _____

3. What is volume?

   _____

   _____

4. Explain why the unit for volume is always cubed.

   _____

   _____

5. Suggest a suitable instrument for measuring the volume of the following objects.

   a. A large rock: _____

   b. A solid brick: _____

   c. A can of beans: _____

6. Calculate the volume of the following object.

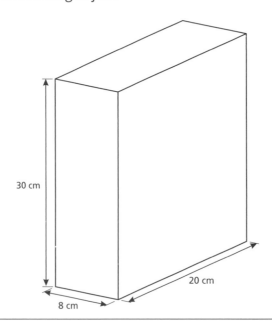

30 cm

20 cm

8 cm

Answer: _____

7. Describe the correct method for reading the volume of liquid in a graduated cylinder.

_____

_____

_____

_____

_____

_____

8. Outline a method for estimating the volume of a €2 coin.

_____

_____

_____

_____

_____

_____

_____

_____

_____

_____

15.4 Accuracy in Measurements

1. Give **two** reasons why scientists collect data for physical quantities.

   _____

   _____

2. Complete the following sentences using the words below.

   | measure | accurate | errors | inaccurate | data |

   A large amount of numbers that have been collected to describe a physical quantity is referred to as a set of _____. Scientists must _____ a physical quantity in a way that ensures it is _____. If a measurement is _____ it results in _____ in the data.

3. **a.** What is a random error?

   _____

   b. Give an example of how a student might make a random error in a measurement.

   _____

   _____

   _____

   c. Suggest how the student could correct this random error.

   _____

   _____

   _____

4. **a.** What is a systematic error?

   _____

   b. Give an example of how a student might make a systematic error in a measurement.

   _____

   _____

   _____

   c. Suggest how the student could correct this systematic error.

   _____

   _____

5. Explain why you should press the zero button before you use an electronic mass balance to measure the mass of an object.

   _____

   _____

   _____

Crossword

Chapter 15: Measuring the Physical World

Across

2. SI unit of mass. (8)
5. SI unit of temperature. (6)
11. Amount of space taken up by an object. (6)
12. SI unit of electric current. (6)
13. Used to measure the thickness of wire. (10)

Down

1. SI unit of power. (4)
3. Used to measure short, curved lines. (10)
4. SI unit of volume. (5, 5)
6. SI unit of force. (6)
7. Amount of space taken up by a two-dimensional shape. (4)
8. Non-typical data value. (7)
9. Anything that takes up space and has a mass. (6)
10. Bowl-shaped appearance of the surface of a liquid in a graduated cylinder. (8)

Energy

16.1 What is Energy?

1. What is the relationship between energy and work?

   _____

   _____

2. State the law of conservation of energy.

   _____

   _____

3. Complete the following table to show how different objects store or possess energy.

Object	Stores/possesses energy in the form of ...
A car rolling down a hill	Kinetic energy
An archer pulling back the bow	
A bowl of cornflakes	
A nucleus of Uranium-236	
The magnet that closes the door of the fridge	
Hot water in a vacuum flask	

4. Distinguish between kinetic energy and potential energy.

   _____

   _____

   _____

5. **a.** Outline how energy is converted from one form to another when a person cycles a bike.

   _____

   _____

   _____

   b. Identify how energy may be dissipated in such an energy conversion.

   _____

   _____

   _____

16.2 Energy Transfers

1. Which of the following energy transfers occur in a torch?

    a. Electrical ⟶ chemical ⟶ light

    b. Chemical ⟶ electrical ⟶ light

    c. Light ⟶ chemical ⟶ electrical

    Answer: _____

2. Explain what is meant by the 'dissipation of energy'. Give **one** example.

    _____

    _____

    _____

    _____

3. **a.** Draw a Sankey diagram to show the following energy transfers in a filament bulb.

    • 600 J of electrical energy

    • 60 J of light energy

    • 540 J of heat energy

    b. Calculate the percentage efficiency of the bulb.

    Answer: _____

16.3 Energy Transfer in the Home

1. What is power?

   _____

2. What unit do electricity supply companies use to report the quantity of electrical energy used by a consumer?

   _____

3. Convert the power of the following appliances to kilowatts.

   a. 800 W coffee maker: _____

   b. 1,000 W iron: _____

   c. 1,600 W microwave: _____

   d. 1,200 W toaster: _____

4. **a.** Calculate how many units of electrical energy (joules) will be converted to thermal and light energy by an electric toaster with a power rating of 1.5 kW that is operational for 60 seconds.

   _____
   | |
   | |
   | |
   | |
   | |
   |_____|

   Answer: _____

   b. What is the total cost to a consumer based on the following usage of the toaster?

   • 60 seconds each morning (Monday to Sunday) over eight weeks.

   • Each unit of electricity is charged at €0.14.

   _____
   | |
   | |
   | |
   | |
   | |
   |_____|

   Answer: _____

5. Outline **three** ways that a homeowner could improve energy efficiency and reduce the cost of their energy bills.

   _____

   _____

   _____

   _____

   _____

   _____

   _____

Crossword

Chapter 16: Energy

Across

7. Transfer of energy from one form to another. (10)

8. Energy of an object due to movement. (7)

11. Unit to describe the power rating of electrical appliances. (9)

13. Certificate stating a home's energy use. (8, 6, 6)

Down

1. Heat energy. (7)

2. Energy in coal, oil and gas. (8)

3. Energy in the nucleus of an atom. (7)

4. Diagram showing all transfers of energy in a process. (6)

5. Energy transfer in non-useful forms. (11)

6. Device used to monitor energy use. (6, 5)

9. Method of preventing energy loss through walls and roof. (10)

10. Energy of an object due to its shape or position. (9)

12. SI unit of energy. (5)

Chapter 17

Motion

17.1 Types of Motion

1. List five types of basic motion.

_____

_____

_____

2. Complete the following table.

Quantity	SI unit of measurement (and symbol)
Distance	
Speed	
Length	
	Second (s)

3. **a.** A student walks at an average speed of 1.4 m/s. Her first class of the day is science. The science laboratory is 105 m from her locker. Calculate how long it will take her to walk from her locker to class.

Answer: _____

b. Draw a distance-time graph to show the student's motion as she moves to her next class, as follows:

- Leaves the door of science lab at 10.20 am and walks 50 m, arriving at the bottom of the stairs after 30 s.
- Waits at the bottom of the stairs for 15 s to let other students pass.
- Climbs up two flights of stairs – a total distance of 15 m in 30 s.
- Walks 75 m to the door of her next class in 35 s.

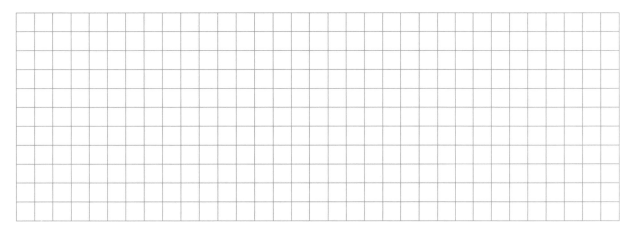

c. At what time did the student arrive at the door of her next class?

_____

d. At which stage in her journey was she travelling at her fastest? Explain your answer.

_____

_____

e. What was her average speed for the entire journey?

Answer: _____

4. Explain the difference between scalar and vector quantities. Give **one** example of each.

_____

_____

_____

_____

17.2 Changing Speeds

1. What is acceleration?

_____

_____

2. **a.** A student walks at an average speed of 1.4 m/s for 10 s. When he hears the bell for the start of class, he starts to accelerate and reaches a faster speed of 2.8 m/s. It takes him 7 s to reach his new speed. Calculate his acceleration.

[   ]

Answer: _____

b. Draw a distance-time graph to show the student's motion if he continues to walk at the new speed of 2.8 m/s for the next 30 s until he arrives at class.

c. At what time did the student arrive at the door of his class?

_____

d. At which stage in his journey was he accelerating? Explain your answer, with reference to the shape of the graph.

_____

_____

_____

_____

3. What term is used to describe the acceleration of a body that is slowing down?

_____

17.3 Forces: Pushes and Pulls

1. What is a force?

   _____

   _____

2. Outline **three** effects of a force.

   _____

   _____

   _____

3. Complete the following table.

Force	Contact or non-contact	Example
		Brakes slowing down cars
Magnetic	Non-contact	
Tension		
Push and pull	Contact	
		Earth orbiting the Sun
Electrostatic		
		Insects walking on water
Support		Buoys floating on water

4. What is an interaction pair? Give **one** example.

   _____

   _____

   _____

5. What instrument is used in a laboratory to measure a force?

   _____

17.4 Forces: Moving Faster and Slower

1. What is equilibrium? Give **one** example of an object in equilibrium.

   _____

   _____

2. Complete the following sentences using the words below.

   > equilibrium   unbalanced   balanced

   Student A and student B are having a tug of war. To begin, both students pull the rope with equal force. They do not move, as the forces are _____. The rope is in a state of _____. Student B begins to exert a greater force, making the forces _____ and causing student A to move.

3. List **three** potential effects of a pair of unbalanced forces acting on an object.

   _____

   _____

   _____

   _____

   _____

4. Identify the pair of equal but opposite forces that cause dynamic equilibrium after a skydiver opens their parachute.

   _____

   _____

   _____

5. Explain why it is harder to walk in an open area on a windy day.

   _____

   _____

   _____

   _____

6. Identify **two** useful effects of friction.

   _____

   _____

7. Outline **two** ways to reduce the nuisance effects of friction.

   _____

   _____

   _____

   _____

17.5 Forces: Changing Shapes

1. What term is used to describe the change in shape of an object due to an applied force acting on the object?

   _____

2. **a.** Outline what happens to a yoga mat each time a person steps on it.

   _____
   _____
   _____
   _____
   _____

   b. Draw a labelled diagram to show the forces in action.

3. Explain the term **reaction force**. Give **one** example.

   _____
   _____
   _____

4. Explain the term **elastic** as applied to objects that experience a force.

   _____
   _____

5. List **three** everyday examples of elastic objects.

   _____
   _____
   _____

6. Explain the term **elastic limit**.

   _____
   _____

17.6 Forces: Pressure

1. What is pressure?
   _____

2. What is the SI unit for pressure?
   _____

3. Calculate the pressure exerted on your school desk by a textbook with a mass of 1.09 kg (approximately equal to a weight of 10.7 N) and a surface area of 0.07 m^2.

   ┌───┐
   │   │
   │   │
   │   │
   │   │
   └───┘

   Answer: _____

4. **a.** Draw a simple graph to show how pressure varies with depth in liquids. Put depth along the x-axis and pressure along the y-axis.

   b. Briefly explain the shape of your graph.
   _____
   _____

5. What is gas pressure?
   _____
   _____

6. Outline how atmospheric pressure influences the concentration of oxygen in the air at different altitudes.
   _____
   _____
   _____
   _____

17.7 Forces: Floating and Sinking

1. What is density?

   _____

2. **a.** What is the SI unit for density?

   _____

   b. Which unit is more commonly used for density?

   _____

3. Calculate the density of whole milk with a mass of 1.035 kg and a volume of 1 L (equal to 1,000 cm^3 or 0.001 m^3).

   Answer: _____

4. Explain why a cork from a bottle floats in water but a glass marble sinks.

   _____
   _____
   _____
   _____
   _____
   _____

5. State Archimedes' principle.

   _____
   _____
   _____
   _____

6. What is the force that causes an object to remain buoyant? In your answer, refer to the relationship between depth and pressure in liquids.

   _____
   _____
   _____
   _____
   _____
   _____
   _____

Crossword

Chapter 17: Energy

Across

2. Ratio of mass to volume. (7)
3. Object that restores its shape when force is removed. (7)
4. Name for a Newton meter. (6, 7)
7. Pressure exerted on an object by air. (11, 8)
8. Quantities with a magnitude and an associated direction. (6)
9. SI unit of force. (6)
10. Force acting upwards on an object in a liquid. (8)
11. Equal and opposite force applied by an object to the weight of another object acting on it. (8)

Down

1. Distance an object travels in a given time. (5)
2. Distance an object travels in a given direction. (12)
5. Method used to reduce the friction between two solids in direct contact. (11)
6. Quantities with a magnitude but no associated direction. (6)

Chapter 18

Magnetism and Electricity

18.1 Magnetism

1. What is a magnet?

   _____

2. List **three** magnetic materials.

   _____

   _____

   _____

3. Complete the following sentences using the words below.

   > repel   north   attract   south

   Magnets have a north pole and a south pole. Like poles _____ each other.
   Unlike poles _____ each other. A _____ pole will attract a south pole.
   A _____ pole will repel a south pole.

4. Distinguish between a magnetic field and magnetic field lines.

   _____

   _____

   _____

   _____

5. Draw a labelled diagram of the magnetic field lines around a bar magnet.

6. Explain how a compass works.

   _____

   _____

   _____

7. Outline **two** uses or benefits of the Earth's magnetic field.

   _____

   _____

18.2 What is Electricity?

1. How do we know that electricity is a form of energy?

_____

_____

_____

2. Can you suggest why most home appliances operate on electricity rather than another energy source?

_____

_____

_____

_____

_____

3. Distinguish between static electricity and current electricity.

_____

_____

_____

_____

_____

4. Complete the table to identify the following substances as conductors or insulators.

| rubber | paper | glass | air | water | iron |

Conductors	Insulators

5. Explain why electrical cables are manufactured with copper wires and plastic casing.

_____

_____

_____

_____

_____

_____

18.3 Static Charges

1. What is static electricity?

_____

_____

_____

2. Complete the following sentences using the words below.

| negative | attracts | repels | positive |

A negative charge _____ a negative charge. A _____ charge attracts a positive charge. A _____ charge repels a positive charge. A positive charge _____ a negative charge.

3. **a.** Draw a labelled diagram to show the transfer of electrons upon rubbing amber with fur.

[diagram box]

b. Is amber a conductor or an insulator? Explain your answer.

_____

_____

_____

c. Is fur a conductor or an insulator? Explain your answer.

_____

_____

_____

4. Using your knowledge of subatomic structure, what can you conclude about an atom that is described as 'electrically neutral'? Make reference to protons, neutrons and electrons in your answer.

_____

_____

_____

_____

_____

18.4 Effects of Static Electricity

1. How do cumulonimbus clouds become charged?

   _____

   _____

   _____

2. Indicate the location of positive and negative charges on the following diagram to show how lightning occurs.

3. Explain how a lightning conductor works.

   _____

   _____

   _____

   _____

4. Explain why you see lightning before you hear thunder.

   _____

   _____

   _____

   _____

5. Outline **two** uses of static electricity.

   _____

   _____

   _____

   _____

   _____

18.5 Electric Circuits

1. Match the circuit symbol to the component it represents.

Circuit symbol		Component	
1.		a.	Motor
2.		b.	Bulb
3.		c.	Ammeter
4.		d.	Switch
5.		e.	Buzzer
6.		f.	Battery

1.	2.	3.	4.	5.	6.

2. Explain the role of a battery in an electric circuit.

_____

_____

_____

_____

_____

_____

3. **a.** Draw a simple buzzer circuit diagram. Include the following components:

- Battery (single cell)
- Ammeter
- Conducting wires
- Switch
- Buzzer

b. Identify **three** energy conversions taking place in this circuit and whether each is useful or non-useful (waste).

Conversion	Useful or non-useful

4. List the **three** effects of an electric current.

_____

_____

_____

18.6 Potential Difference and Voltage

1. What is potential difference?

   _____

   _____

   _____

2. Which component is used to measure potential difference in a circuit?

   _____

   _____

   _____

3. Explain what happens to the energy carried by electrons (gained from a cell or battery) as they pass through a buzzer.

   _____

   _____

   _____

   _____

4. Complete the following sentences using the words below.

electrical	negative	potential	positive	chemical

   Current flows from the _____ to the _____ terminal of a battery.
   Batteries are sources of electrical _____ energy. They transfer
   energy into _____ energy.

5. Using the law of conservation of energy and the law of conservation of mass, comment on the accuracy of the statement 'Batteries run out because they lose both their energy and their charge.'

   _____

   _____

   _____

   _____

   _____

   _____

   _____

6. What is the difference between a primary cell and a secondary cell?

   _____

   _____

   _____

   _____

18.7 Series and Parallel Circuits

1. **a.** Draw a circuit diagram with two buzzers in series. Include a switch and a battery.

    b. If a fault developed with one of the buzzers, what would happen to the other buzzer? Explain your answer.

    _____

    _____

    _____

    _____

2. **a.** Draw a circuit diagram with three bulbs in parallel. Include a switch and a battery.

    b. If a fault developed with one of the bulbs, what would happen to the other bulbs? Explain your answer.

    _____

    _____

    _____

    _____

3. Label the missing current and voltage values in the following series circuit diagram.

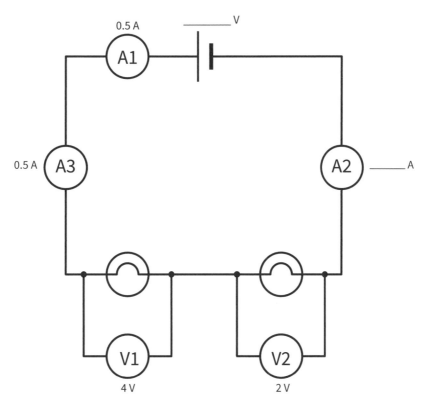

4. Label the missing current and voltage values in the following parallel circuit diagram.

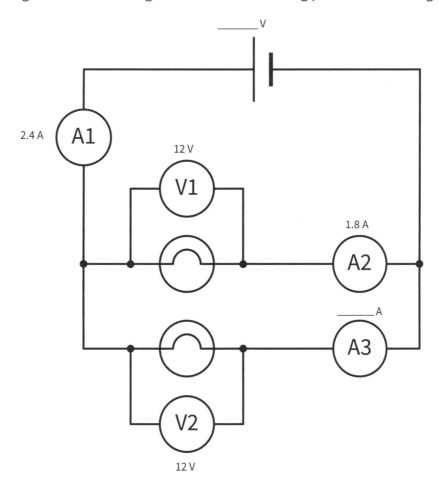

18.8 Resistance

1. What is electrical resistance?

_____

_____

2. What is the SI unit for electrical resistance?

_____

3. **a.** Calculate the resistance of the bulb in the following circuit diagram.

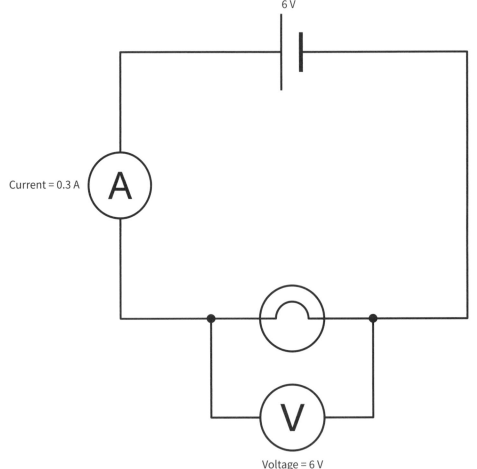

Answer: _____

b. Suggest a way to reduce the current from 0.3 A to 0.15 A that involves changing only one component in the circuit. Show your calculations.

4. Identify **two** uses of resistance.

5. List **three** factors that affect how much a resistor slows down moving charges.

18.9 Electricity in the Home

1. Explain why it is possible to turn one electrical home appliance off while others continue to operate.

   _____

   _____

   _____

   _____

2. Calculate the electrical power of the following appliances.

   a. A microwave connected to a 230 V mains supply with a current of 4 A.

   Answer: _____

   _____

   b. A hair dryer connected to a 220 V mains supply with a current of 10 A.

   Answer: _____

   _____

   c. A tumble dryer connected to a 240 V mains supply with a current of 11 A.

   Answer: _____

   _____

3. Distinguish between alternating current (a.c) and direct current (d.c).

   _____

   _____

   _____

   _____

   _____

4. Draw a circuit diagram of a diode in forward bias. Include a battery, a switch and a motor.

5. Match the part of the plug to its function.

Part		Function	
1.	Fuse	**a.**	Carries electrical current away from the appliance
2.	Live wire	**b.**	Draws a current through the plug in the event of a fault
3.	Plastic outer cable	**c.**	Prevents the appliance receiving too much current
4.	Neutral wire	**d.**	Carries electrical current to the appliance
5.	Earth wire	**e.**	Insulates the wires

1.	2.	3.	4.	5.

Crossword

Chapter 18: Magnetism and Electricity

Across

1. Component that measures resistance. (8)
3. Substances that allow charged particles to flow through them freely. (10)
5. Type of cloud associated with thunder. (12)
6. Circuit with components connected in different branches. (8)
8. Component that measures electric current. (7)
9. Two or more cells connected together. (7)
10. Component that slows down moving charges. (8)
11. SI unit for voltage. (5)
13. SI unit for electric current. (6)
14. Small magnet the moves freely to show direction. (7)
15. Circuit with components connected in a single loop. (6)

Down

2. Materials that are attracted to magnets. (8, 9)
4. Ends of a magnet where the magnetic force is strongest. (5)
5. A flow of charge. (7)
7. Colours in the sky caused by the deflection of cosmic rays by the Earth's magnetic field. (7)
12. Component that allows current to flow in one direction only. (5)

Chapter 19

Seeing, Hearing, Feeling

19.1 Bouncing Light

1. Tick the correct column to identify which statements are true and which are false.

	True	False
Light travels in straight lines		
Light cannot travel through a vacuum		
Light can travel through opaque materials		
Light can travel through transparent materials		
Light cannot be converted into other forms of energy		
Light can move things		

2. **a.** What is diffuse reflection?

_____

_____

_____

_____

   b. Draw a labelled diagram to show diffuse reflection off a rough surface.

3. **a.** What is regular reflection?

_____

_____

_____

_____

b. Draw a labelled diagram to show regular reflection off a smooth surface.

4. List **three** everyday uses of a plane mirror.

_____

_____

_____

19.2 Bending Light

1. What is refraction?

   _____

   _____

   _____

2. Draw a labelled diagram to show how light travels into and out of a glass block.

3. Identify **two** everyday items that work due to their ability to refract light.

   _____

   _____

   _____

4. Describe and explain **one** nuisance effect of refraction (e.g. misjudging the depth of a swimming pool).

   _____

   _____

   _____

5. Label the parts of the eye.

19.3 Splitting Light

1. What is dispersion?

   _____

   _____

   _____

2. Complete the following sentences using the words below.

   > absorb   spectrum   primary   prism
   >
   > white   reflect   secondary   orange

   The colours that make up _____ light are red, _____, yellow, green, blue, indigo and violet. Together, these colours are known as a _____ . This can be seen using a _____ .

   Red, green and blue are _____ colours. When two of these colours combine, they produce _____ colours.

   Objects _____ the colours in white light except their own colour, which they _____ .

3. Explain how we see:

   a. white objects: _____

   _____

   _____

   b. black objects: _____

   _____

   _____

4. Distinguish between the roles of rods and cones in the human eye.

   _____

   _____

   _____

   _____

   _____

5. Predict what would happen if you stacked three filters (red, green and blue) on top of each other and placed them in front of a white light source. Explain your answer.

   _____

   _____

   _____

   _____

   _____

   _____

19.4 Sound

1. What is sound?

   _____

   _____

   _____

2. Outline how a person can hear a guitar being played across room.

   _____

   _____

   _____

   _____

   _____

3. What is the speed of sound in air?

   _____

4. Complete the following sentences using the words below.

   ┌───┐
   │   pitch   amplitude   frequency   │
   └───┘

   The _____ of a sound wave is how fast it is moving. The faster the sound wave moves, the
   higher its _____ will be. The loudness of a sound wave depends on its _____ .
   The higher it is, the louder the sound wave is.

5. Why it is important to wear earplugs at a rock concert? Explain your answer with reference to
   decibels.

   _____

   _____

   _____

   _____

   _____

6. **a.** Draw a high-frequency sound wave.

b. Draw a low-frequency wave.

19.5 Heat Transfer

1. What is heat?

   _____

   _____

2. Match the methods of heat transfer to their descriptions.

Method of heat transfer		Description	
1.	Convection	a.	Transfer of heat through vibrating particles in a solid
2.	Conduction	b.	Transfer of heat in the form of waves
3.	Radiation	c.	Transfer of heat via a current in a liquid or gas

1.	2.	3.

3. Complete the following diagram to show the transfer of heat by convection currents in a liquid.

Water

Coloured dye
heated by candle

4. Using your knowledge of radiation, explain the following scenarios.

   a. Wearing a white T-shirt instead of a black T-shirt on the hottest day of the year.

   _____

   _____

   _____

   _____

   b. Painting the surfaces of home radiators in white metallic paint.

   _____

   _____

   _____

   _____

   _____

19.6 Effects of Heat

1. What is the SI unit of temperature?

2. How is temperature measured in a laboratory?

3. Name the typical unit used to report temperatures in:

   a. Ireland and the rest of Europe: _____

   b. the USA: _____

4. Distinguish between heat and temperature.

5. Tick the correct column to identify which statements are true and which are false.

	True	False
When a solid is heated it expands		
When a gas is heated it contracts		
When water is cooled below 4 °C it expands		
When a solid is cooled it contracts		
When a gas is cooled it contracts		

6. Explain why concrete footpaths are poured as a series of small, separate sections instead of as one large section.

Chapter 19: Seeing, Hearing, Feeling

Across

2. Speed of a sound wave. (8)
7. Transfer of heat in infrared waves. (9)
8. Unit of measurement for sound. (8)
11. Broken when an object travels faster than the speed of sound. (5, 7)
12. Colours that make up white light. (8)

Down

1. Device that shows how light can move things. (7, 10)
3. Photosensitive layer of nerve cells at the back of the eye. (6)
4. Triangular glass object that disperses light to form a spectrum. (5)
5. Device used to measure temperature. (11)
6. Light reflected off a rough surface in all directions. (7)
7. Light bouncing off a surface. (10)
9. Light bending as it passes from one medium to another. (10)
10. Transfer of heat through vibration of particles. (10)

The Modern Physical World

20.1 The Information Age

1. Distinguish between an analogue signal and a digital signal.

   _____

   _____

   _____

2. Outline how two people can communicate via a landline telephone. Include the following terms: microphone, vibrations of sound waves, analogue signal, digital signal, processor and loudspeaker.

   _____

   _____

   _____

   _____

   _____

   _____

3. Define the following terms:

   a. binary: _____

   b. bit: _____

   c. byte: _____

4. Match the wave type to devices that transmit them.

Wave type		Devices	
1.	Radio waves	a.	Cameras
2.	Visible waves	b.	Remote controls
3.	Microwaves	c.	Mobile phones
4.	X-ray	d.	Fluorescent lights
5.	Infrared waves	e.	Wi-Fi hubs
6.	Ultraviolet	f.	Radiotherapy machines
7.	Gamma ray	g.	Baggage scanners

1.	2.	3.	4.	5.	6.	7.

5. Outline **one** positive and **one** negative effect of the internet.

   _____

   _____

   _____

   _____

20.2 Physics and Health

1. Draw a graph to show how the resistance of a thermistor varies with temperature. Label the *x*-axis as temperature and the *y*-axis as resistance.

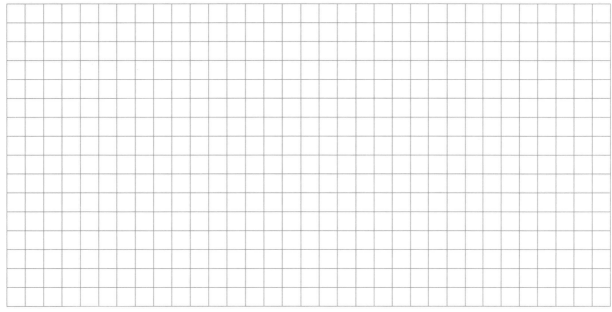

2. Explain how a pacemaker works.

_____

_____

_____

3. **a.** What does the acronym MRI stand for?

_____

 b. Explain how an MRI machine is used.

_____

_____

_____

4. How is ultrasound used in hospitals?

_____

_____

_____

5. Explain the function of optical fibres in endoscopes. Refer to both refraction and total internal reflection of light.

_____

_____

_____

_____

_____

20.3 Fast Physics

1. What is a particle accelerator?

_____

_____

_____

_____

2. What type of energy is converted into other forms when particles collide?

_____

3. Explain how a cathode ray tube (CRT) operates.

_____

_____

_____

_____

_____

4. Explain how an X-ray machine is used in hospitals to assess potential bone fractures or breaks.

_____

_____

_____

_____

_____

_____

5. Outline the three phases of operation of the Large Hadron Collider (LHC) at CERN in Geneva, Switzerland.

_____

_____

_____

_____

_____

_____

_____

6. Why was the discovery of the Higgs boson particle significant?

_____

_____

_____

_____

_____

Crossword

Chapter 20: The Modern Physical World

Across

1. Indicators of a person's health. (5, 5)
5. Device that transmits a large voltage to 'kick-start' the heart into beating with a normal rhythm. (13)
6. Loop of wire around an iron core. (13)
8. Device used to look inside the body. (9)
10. Device whose resistance decreases when heated. (9)
11. Signal with varying values. (8)

Down

2. Globally interconnected computer networks. (8)
3. Particle thought to be responsible for transforming energy into mass at the dawn of time. (5, 5)
4. Only Irish scientist to win a Nobel Prize in Physics. (6, 6)
7. Values that make up a digital signal. (6)
9. Signal with only two values (1 or 0). (7)

Earth and Space

Chapter 21

Space

21.1 Origins of the Universe

1. Explain the difference between the terms **geocentric** and **heliocentric**.

   _____

   _____

2. Put the following in order of size by numbering them 1 to 5.

   Galaxy ☐

   Star ☐

   Solar system ☐

   Universe ☐

   Planet ☐

3. What are the main ideas of the Big Bang Theory?

   _____

   _____

   _____

   _____

   _____

4. How long ago was the Big Bang?

   _____

5. List, in chronological order, **three** things that have happened since the Big Bang.

   _____

   _____

   _____

   _____

6. What observations did Edwin Hubble make about our universe?

   _____

   _____

   _____

7. State and explain **two** reasons why our understanding of the universe has changed over time.

   _____

   _____

   _____

   _____

   _____

21.2 Celestial Bodies

1. Read the following sentences and explain the terms in bold.

   The Earth is a **planet** with one **moon**. It is found in the **solar system**. The solar system is part of the Milky Way **galaxy**.

   Planet: _____

   _____

   Moon: _____

   _____

   Solar system: _____

   _____

   Galaxy: _____

   _____

2. What **three** conditions must a celestial body meet to be considered a planet?

   _____

   _____

   _____

   _____

   _____

3. State **one** difference between an asteroid and a comet.

   _____

   _____

4. What element is involved in the nuclear reactions that take place in a star?

   _____

5. What is a light year?

   _____

   _____

6. Name **two** places in the solar system where comets are found.

   _____

   _____

7. Explain the location of a comet's tail as it travels **towards** and **away** from the Sun.

   Towards the Sun: _____

   _____

   Away from the Sun: _____

   _____

21.3 The Planets in Our Solar System

1. Explain the difference between a terrestrial planet and a gas giant and give **one** example of each.

_____

_____

_____

_____

2. Match the planets to their descriptions.

Planet	Description
1. Jupiter	a. Planet with a bright system of rings
2. Earth	b. Red planet
3. Venus	c. Hottest planet
4. Saturn	d. Planet with the longest day
5. Uranus	e. Largest planet
6. Mars	f. Planet with the chemicals to support life
7. Mercury	g. Planet with an atmosphere of cold methane gas
8. Neptune	h. Planet that is tilted on its side as it rotates around the Sun

1.	2.	3.	4.	5.	6.	7.	8.

3. Draw a labelled diagram to show the planets and the Sun in the solar system.

4. Name **three** moons in the solar system.

_____

_____

5. What is gravity?

_____

_____

6. What **two** factors need to be considered when working out the weight of an object?

_____

_____

7. The table below shows data for some of the largest objects in our solar system, including the Sun, the planets, some dwarf planets and some moons.

In each case the radius, mass and surface gravities of the object are relative to those of the Earth. (For example, the Sun's relative radius of 109 means that its radius is 109 times the radius of the Earth.)

Object	Type of object	Relative mass	Relative radius	Surface gravity
Sun	Star	333,000	109	28.0
Jupiter	Planet	318	11.0	2.53
Earth	Planet	1	1	1
Venus	Planet	0.815	0.950	0.905
Mars	Planet	0.107	0.532	0.38
Ganymede	Moon of Jupiter	0.0248	0.413	0.15
Titan	Moon of Saturn	0.0225	0.404	0.14
Mercury	Planet	0.0553	0.383	0.38
Callisto	Moon of Jupiter	0.0180	0.378	0.126

Use the table to suggest a relationship between the relative mass of an object and its surface gravity. Use figures from the table to support your answer.

_____

_____

_____

_____

_____

_____

_____

_____

Chapter 21: Space

Across

1. Non-contact force that is greater on Earth than on the Moon. (7)
3. Planet with the Great Dark Spot. (7)
5. Planets mostly made up of hydrogen and helium. (3, 6)
7. First stage in the life cycle of a small star. (6)
9. Region in space where an object feels a force. (5, 5)
10. Natural satellite. (4)
11. Explosion thought to have formed the universe. (3, 4)
12. Celestial body that was reclassified as a dwarf planet. (5)
13. Plato and Aristotle's theory of the universe. (10)
14. Shape of our galaxy. (6)

Down

2. Spins in the opposite direction to the other planets in the solar system. (5)
4. First spacecraft to land on a comet. (6, 6)
6. Latin term meaning 'land'. (5)
8. Celestial body made up of dust, ice, small rocks and gas that orbits the Sun. (5)
10. Smallest planet. (7)
14. Closest star to the Earth. (3)

Earth

22.1 The Structure of the Earth

1. Approximately how long ago was the Earth formed?

_____

2. Label the parts of the following diagram that shows the structure of the Earth.

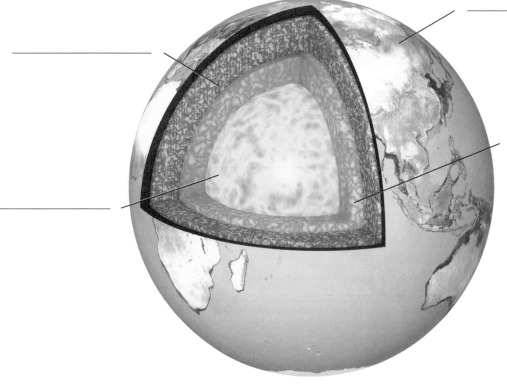

3. Match the layers of the Earth to their descriptions.

Layer	Description
1. Mantle	a. Liquid layer of iron and nickel
2. Crust	b. Solid rock and magma
3. Inner core	c. Supports life in oceans and continents
4. Outer core	d. Solid layer of iron and nickel

1.	2.	3.	4.

4. What is seismology?

_____

_____

_____

5. a. What is plate tectonics?

_____

_____

_____

b. What natural phenomena are caused by plate tectonics?

_____

_____

_____

_____

6. a. Match the types of rocks found in the Earth's crust to the description of how they are formed.

Rock type		Description of formation
1. Igneous	**a.**	Other rock types become harder due to high temperatures and pressure
2. Sedimentary	**b.**	Magma from a volcano breaks through the Earth's surface, cools and solidifies
3. Metamorphic	**c.**	Rock particles and dead plants and animals build up over millions of years

1.	2.	3.

b. Name **one** example of each type of rock.

Igneous: _____

Sedimentary: _____

Metamorphic: _____

22.2 The Cycling of Matter

1. What do nutrient cycles describe?

_____

_____

2. Complete the following sentences using the words below.

> combustion   respiration   source   sink   photosynthesis

Anything that takes carbon out of the atmosphere is a carbon _____. During _____, plants take carbon out of the atmosphere in the form of carbon dioxide.

Anything that releases carbon into the atmosphere is known as a carbon _____. During _____, organisms release carbon into the atmosphere in the form of carbon dioxide.

Carbon is also released into the atmosphere during the _____ of fossil fuels. Increased carbon dioxide in the atmosphere is responsible for global warming.

3. Outline the role of decomposers in the carbon cycle.

_____

_____

_____

_____

_____

4. Explain why nitrogen is an important element for life.

_____

_____

_____

_____

_____

5. Match the different types of bacteria to the roles they play in the nitrogen cycle.

Bacteria		Role in nitrogen cycle	
1.	Decomposers	a.	Change nitrogen in the air into nitrates suitable for use by plants
2.	Nitrogen-fixing bacteria	b.	Break down nitrates in soil and return it to the atmosphere as nitrogen gas
3.	Denitrifying bacteria	c.	Return nitrogen to the soil as ammonium by breaking down dead organisms

1.	2.	3.

22.3 Water

1. Tick the correct column to identify which statements are true and which are false.

	True	False
Water is a compound of hydrogen and oxygen atoms		
Water covers 30% of the Earth's surface		
Water freezes at 0 °C		
Water is essential for life on Earth		
Water boils at 99 °C		
Water expands as it freezes		
Water is a bad solvent		

2. What are the three states of water?

_____

_____

3. Label the parts of the following diagram to show the processes in the water cycle.

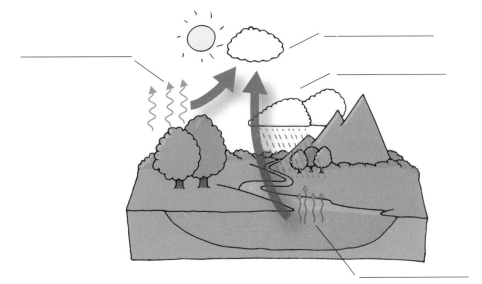

4. Put the stages of water treatment in the correct order by numbering them 1 to 5.

Chlorination   ☐

Settling   ☐

Fluoridation   ☐

Filtration   ☐

Screening   ☐

5. What is electrolysis?

_____

_____

_____

22.4 The Atmosphere

1. What is the atmosphere?

_____

2. a. Identify the **two** main gases that make up the Earth's atmosphere.

_____

b. Explain why the composition of air can change.

_____

_____

3. Complete the following table to outline **three** properties and **three** uses for oxygen and carbon dioxide.

Gas	Properties	Uses
Oxygen		
Carbon dioxide		

4. Match the layers of the atmosphere to their descriptions.

Layer	Description
1. Stratosphere	a. Lowest layer of the atmosphere, in which the Earth's weather systems form
2. Troposphere	b. Hottest layer of the Earth's atmosphere, in which aurorae are visible
3. Thermosphere	c. Contains the ozone layer, which protects the Earth from harmful UV rays
4. Mesosphere	d. Highest layer of the atmosphere, where Earth meets space
5. Exosphere	e. Coldest layer of the atmosphere, in which shooting stars can be seen

1.	2.	3.	4.	5.

5. Explain how changes in atmospheric pressure influence the weather close to the Earth's surface.

_____

_____

_____

Crossword

Chapter 22: Earth

Across

1. Step of the water treatment process when chlorine is added. (12)
6. Lines on a weather chart that join areas of equal pressure. (7)
7. Type of rock formed from other rocks over time by high temperature and pressure. (11)
9. Hot molten or semi-molten rock mixture. (5)
10. Scale that describes the magnitude of an earthquake. (7)
11. Scientist who studies the weather. (13)
12. Exists in the stratosphere to protect Earth from UV rays. (5, 5)
13. Step of the water cycle when clouds form. (12)
14. Device used to measure changes in atmospheric pressure. (9)

Down

2. Equipment used in the electrolysis of water. (7, 10)
3. Outermost layer of the Earth. (5)
4. Part of the Earth that can support life. (9)
5. Solution that turns milky in a positive test for carbon dioxide. (9)
8. Large chunks of the Earth's crust that float on the mantle. (6)

The Interaction Between Earth and Space

23.1 The Earth and the Sun

1. Give **two** examples of everyday objects that are transparent, translucent or opaque.

Transparent	
Translucent	
Opaque	

2. Explain how shadows form on a sunny day.

_____
_____
_____
_____
_____

3. What does the term **axis** mean?

_____
_____
_____
_____

4. Explain why we experience different seasons on Earth.

_____
_____
_____
_____
_____
_____
_____

5. Look at the diagram below, which shows Earth's position relative to the Sun.

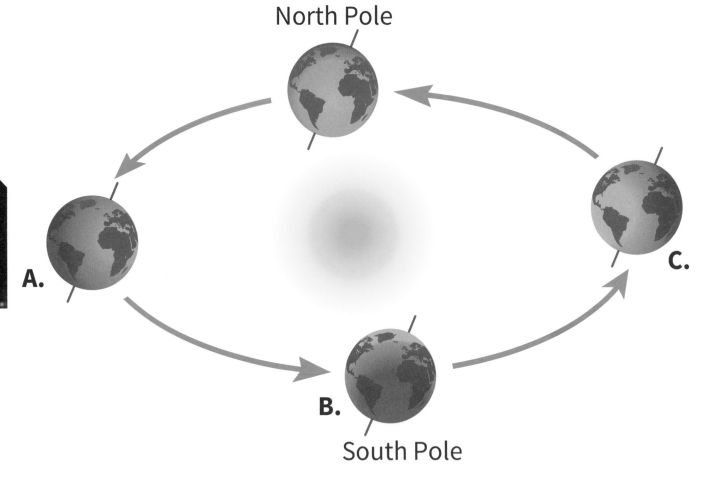

North Pole

A.

C.

B.

South Pole

a. At position B, what season is it in the Northern Hemisphere?

_____

b. At position C, what season is it in the Southern Hemisphere?

_____

c. At position A, which hemisphere will have the longest days?

_____

d. At position C, which pole will have darkness for 24 hours?

_____

e. At position A, which pole will have daylight for 24 hours?

_____

23.2 The Earth and the Moon

1. Put the phases of the Moon in the correct order by numbering them 1 to 8.

   First quarter ☐

   Crescent moon ☐

   New moon ☐

   Waning gibbous ☐

   Full moon ☐

   Crescent moon ☐

   Waxing gibbous ☐

2. Draw a diagram to show the arrangement of the Earth, Moon and Sun during a solar eclipse.

3. Draw a diagram to show the arrangement of the Earth, Moon and Sun during a lunar eclipse.

4. Explain the difference between the following terms.

   a. Waxing and waning: _____

   _____

   b. New moon and full moon: _____

   _____

   c. Crescent moon and a gibbous moon: _____

   _____

155

Crossword

Chapter 23: The Interaction Between Earth and Space

Across

5. Eclipse when the Earth is between the Sun and Moon. (5)

8. Division of the year characterised by changes in weather and hours of daylight. (6)

9. Darkest part of the shadow during an eclipse. (5)

10. Direction of the Earth's orbit around the Sun. (13)

12. Time taken for Earth to orbit the Sun. (4)

Down

1. Shape of the Earth's orbit around the Sun. (10)

2. Object that allows only some light to pass through. (11)

3. Radiation emitted by the Sun. (11)

4. The Moon appears to grow. (6)

6. An object light cannot pass through. (6)

7. Number of Moon phases. (5)

11. Eclipse when the Moon is between the Sun and Earth. (5)

13. Imaginary line linking the North and South Poles. (4)

Chapter 24

Sources of Energy

24.1 Our Current Energy Needs

1. What are fossil fuels?

   _____

2. Distinguish between renewable and non-renewable energy sources.

   _____
   _____
   _____
   _____
   _____

3. **a.** Ireland relies heavily on fossil fuels for energy. Give **three** disadvantages of this situation.

   _____
   _____
   _____
   _____
   _____

   b. Suggest **two** alternative sources of energy for Ireland and justify your suggestions.

   _____
   _____
   _____
   _____
   _____
   _____

4. Describe the energy changes that take place when fossil fuels are used in a power plant to generate electricity.

   _____
   _____
   _____
   _____
   _____
   _____
   _____
   _____
   _____

5. Give a brief description of how **two** renewable energy sources generate energy.

_____

_____

_____

_____

_____

6. Complete the following table to show the conditions required to generate energy from the renewable sources listed.

Source	Necessary conditions
Solar energy	
Wave energy	
Wind energy	

7. Outline **two** ways that the world's energy needs could be provided for without any further damage to our environment.

_____

_____

_____

_____

_____

_____

_____

_____

_____

_____

24.2 Nuclear Energy

1. Name a fuel source for a nuclear power plant.

   _____

2. Outline **two** advantages of nuclear energy.

   _____
   _____
   _____
   _____

3. Explain **two** reasons why some people are opposed to nuclear energy.

   _____
   _____
   _____
   _____

4. Outline why it is more desirable to use nuclear fusion reactions than nuclear fission reactions to generate energy.

   _____
   _____
   _____
   _____

5. Draw a diagram to show how nuclear fission takes place.

6. Draw a diagram to show how nuclear fusion takes place.

24.3 Smart Technologies

1. What is a nanometre?

   _____

2. Arrange the following objects from smallest to largest by numbering them 1 to 5.

   DNA (~2 nanometres) ☐

   Hair (~50,000 nanometres) ☐

   Red blood cell (~7,000 nanometres) ☐

   1 cent piece (~15,000,000 nanometres) ☐

   Bacteria (~5,000 nanometres) ☐

3. **a.** What is graphene?

   _____

   _____

   b. Name a source of graphene.

   _____

4. Complete the following table by calculating the length of the objects in nanometres.

   > 1 centimetre = 10,000,000 nanometres

Object	Length (mm or cm)	Length (nm)
Paperclip	3 cm	
Ruler	30 cm	
Ball-point pen	15 cm	
Catalyst textbook	29.5 cm	
Metre stick	100 cm	

5. Explain how solar cells can improve technological advances.

   _____

   _____

   _____

   _____

Crossword

Chapter 24: Sources of Energy

Across

3. Element used in nuclear fission. (7)

4. Element used in nuclear fusion. (8)

7. Energy sources formed from the remains of plants and animals. (6, 5)

9. Science of the very small. (14)

11. Biological materials used as fuel. (7)

12. Controlled or uncontrolled series of reactions in nuclear fission. (5, 8)

13. Machine used in the production of wave energy. (7)

Down

1. Power generated when water is released from a dam. (13)

2. Nuclear reaction that combines two small nuclei into a single large nucleus. (6)

5. Fuel source that will not run out. (9)

6. Nuclear reaction that splits a large nucleus into two smaller nuclei. (6)

8. Device that converts light energy from the Sun into electrical energy. (5, 4)

10. One-atom-thick sheet of carbon. (8)

Chapter 25

A Sustainable World

25.1 The Growth of the Human Population

1. When do scientists believe the first organisms appeared on Earth?

   _____

2. How long do scientists believe humans have lived on Earth?

   _____

3. Outline **three** reasons for the huge increase in the size of the human population in the last 300 years.

   _____

   _____

   _____

   _____

4. Outline **three** possible negative impacts on the planet of a growing global population.

   _____

   _____

   _____

   _____

   _____

5. Some scientific research has suggested that today's young people may not live as long as their parents' generation.

   a. What information do you think this research might be based on?

   _____

   _____

   _____

   b. What steps might be taken to prevent this predicted trend?

   _____

   _____

   _____

   _____

   _____

25.2 Human Impact on the Earth

1. a. What is extinction?

_____

b. Outline **three** human behaviours that contribute to a species becoming extinct.

_____

_____

_____

_____

c. Outline **three** ways to help prevent a species becoming extinct.

_____

_____

_____

_____

2. What is pollution?

_____

_____

3. Complete the following table to outline **two** causes and **two** effects of the main sources of pollution.

Source of Pollution	Cause(s)	Effect(s)
Agricultural		
Industrial		
Domestic		

4. **a.** Explain the term **global warming**.

_____

_____

_____

   b. Identify the major cause of global warming.

_____

_____

_____

5. **a.** Identify **three** effects of acid rain.

_____

_____

_____

_____

_____

_____

   b. Identify **three** ways of addressing the causes of acid rain.

_____

_____

_____

_____

_____

_____

_____

_____

25.3 Meeting the Challenges Facing the Earth

1. What is sustainability?

_____

_____

2. Complete the following table to outline **one** advantage and **one** disadvantage of each method of waste management.

Method	Advantage	Disadvantage
Landfill sites		
Incineration		
Waste minimisation		

3. Outline the role of bacteria in waste management.

_____

_____

_____

4. Outline **two** ways that the government can promote sustainability.

_____

_____

_____

_____

5. Outline **five** steps that an individual can take to live sustainably.

_____

_____

_____

_____

_____

_____

_____

6. What is reforestation?

_____

_____

Crossword

Chapter 25: A Sustainable World

Across

1. Breakdown of organic matter to return nutrients to soil. (10)
4. Planting crops in order to protect the soil. (4, 8)
6. Meeting our own needs while protecting the needs of future generations. (14)
8. Damage caused to land due to over farming or overgrazing. (15)
9. Harmful rain water with a pH of less than 5.5. (4, 4)
10. Destruction of large areas of forest. (13)
11. Careless disposal of rubbish. (9)
12. How society deals with waste. (5, 10)

Down

2. Leading cause of climate change. (6, 7)
3. Protection of Earth's natural resources. (12)
5. Burning waste to reduce its volume. (12)
7. Sudden rise in algae in rivers and lakes caused by enrichment. (5, 5)

Chapter 26

Space Travel

26.1 Space Flight

1. What was the Space Race?

   _____

   _____

   _____

   _____

2. What is the difference between an astronaut and a cosmonaut?

   _____

   _____

3. What does NASA stand for?

   _____

4. Outline the difference between a rocket and a shuttle.

   _____

   _____

   _____

   _____

5. What important information does the International Space Station (ISS) provide?

   _____

   _____

   _____

   _____

6. How many times in one day does the ISS orbit the Earth?

   _____

7. Draw a diagram to show the forces that occur when a spacecraft is launched.

26.2 Looking at the Night Sky: Light Telescopes

1. What is an astronomer?

   _____

   _____

2. Draw a diagram to illustrate how light refracts through a convex lens.

   [blank box]

3. Draw a diagram to illustrate how light refracts through a concave lens.

   [blank box]

4. **a.** List the **three** types of light telescope.

   _____

   _____

   b. Explain how **one** of the light telescopes you have named works.

   _____

   _____

   _____

   _____

   _____

5. What is a constellation?

   _____

   _____

26.3 Looking at the Night Sky: Radio Telescopes

1 What is a wave?

_____

_____

2. Explain how a radio telescope works.

_____

_____

_____

_____

3. Draw a diagram to show the following features of a wave: amplitude, wavelength, crest and trough.

_____

4. Explain why radio telescopes are more useful than light telescopes.

_____

_____

_____

_____

5. List **three** types of waves present in space.

_____

_____

6. Explain why radio waves can be viewed using telescopes but gamma waves, for example, cannot.

_____

_____

_____

_____

26.4 Space and the Future

1. What is the general purpose of space missions?

   _____

   _____

   _____

2. Match the types of space mission to their descriptions.

Type of mission		Description	
1.	Flyby	**a.**	Circles a celestial body
2.	Robotic lander	**b.**	A spacecraft passes a celestial body on its way to another destination
3.	Human	**c.**	Lands a spacecraft in a pre-mapped location
4.	Orbiter	**d.**	People are sent to the celestial body

1.	2.	3.	4.

3. Outline the findings of NASA's Curiosity Mars rover.

   _____

   _____

   _____

   _____

4. What is commercial space travel?

   _____

   _____

   _____

5. Outline **three** ways that scientists search for evidence of life in the universe.

   _____

   _____

   _____

   _____

   _____

   _____

6. Outline **three** hazards humans would face living in space.

   _____

   _____

   _____

   _____

   _____

Chapter 26: Space Travel

Across

5. Lenses that converge light. (6)
6. NASA mission that landed humans on the Moon. (6)
8. First person to walk on the Moon. (4, 9)
11. Bottom of wave. (6)
12. Greatest displacement of a wave from its undisplaced position. (9)
13. Type of telescope that uses lenses and mirrors. (5)
14. Number of waves that pass a point in one second. (9)

Down

1. Unmanned spacecraft that gathers information. (5)
2. Distance from the crest of one wave to another. (10)
3. Lenses that diverge light. (7)
4. Group of stars in a pattern. (12)
5. Rover sent to Mars. (9)
7. Top of a wave. (5)
9. Element in which the Voyager records are plated. (4)
10. First Russian satellite in space. (7)